DATA MEETS DECISIONS

A Project Manager's Guide to Analytics with Real-Life Stories

AF797356

SHARIFUL HAQUE, PMP® | KAZI SANWARUL AZIM, PMP®
DHIRAJ KUMAR AKULA, PMP® | KHALED AL-SAMAD
MD. NADIL KHAN, PMP® | MD MOHAIMINUL HASAN, PMP®
NUR MOHAMMAD | ROKSANA AKTER

Data Meets Decisions

A Project Manager's Guide to Analytics with Real-Life Stories

By

Shariful Haque, PMP® | Kazi Sanwarul Azim, PMP® | Dhiraj Kumar Akula, PMP® | Khaled Al-Samad | MD. Nadil Khan, PMP® | MD Mohaiminul Hasan, PMP® | Nur Mohammad | Roksana Akter

Copyright © 2025 Sharif -ul- Haque

All Rights Reserved

No part of this book may be reproduced or transmitted, downloaded, distributed, reverse engineered, or stored in or introduced into any information storage and retrieval system, in any form or by any means, including photocopying and recording, whether electronic or mechanical, now known or hereinafter invented without permission in writing from the publisher.

First Edition: 2025

Published in United States of America

Publisher: US Publishing Experts

Paperback ISBN: 978-1-966418-39-9

DEDICATION

To the project managers who dare to ask "Why?" and to the data analysts who strive to answer "How?"

This book is dedicated to the bridge-builders—those who see beyond the rows and columns of data to find the human stories and strategic decisions that drive progress. May this work empower you to turn insight into action and complexity into clarity.

PREFACE

In the rapidly evolving landscape of modern business, the divide between Project Management and Data Analytics has long been a barrier to true efficiency. For years, project managers have relied on intuition and experience, while data analysts have focused on algorithms and models. But as we step further into the digital age, these two worlds are colliding—and collaborating—in ways that are transforming industries.

Data Meets Decisions was born out of a necessity to demystify analytics for the non-technical leader. It is not just a technical manual; it is a narrative of transition. We wanted to create a guide that speaks the language of the project manager while introducing the powerful vocabulary of data science.

Through real-life stories, practical examples, and a focus on actionable insights, this book aims to equip you with the tools to navigate this new terrain. Whether you are a seasoned PMP® holder or a newcomer to the field, the integration of data into your decision-making process is no longer an option—it is a requirement for success.

Welcome to the future of project management.

ACKNOWLEDGMENTS

This book is the result of a collective effort that spans continents, industries, and disciplines. It would not have been possible without the unwavering support of our families, who stood by us through long nights of writing and revision.

We are deeply grateful to the academic and professional communities that have shaped our understanding of these topics. A special thanks goes to our colleagues and mentors who challenged our ideas and pushed us to refine our thinking.

To the project management community: thank you for your continuous pursuit of excellence. Your challenges and triumphs are the inspiration behind every chapter of this book.

Table of Contents

LET'S GET STARTED

INTRODUCTION

...■...■...

In the modern world of hyper connection and abundance of data, organizations are no longer constrained by the lack of information; on the contrary, they are overwhelmed by it. Any project generates a flow of numbers, reports, dashboards, emails, logs, and metrics. However, in spite of this richness, there are numerous project decisions which are made due to intuition, patchy knowledge, or obsolete glimpses of reality. The result is well known: lateness, overruns, stakeholders out of sync and results which were not in line with strategic intent. Data Meets Decisions was also authored to fill this very gap, not by turning project managers into data scientists, but by enabling project managers to think, lead, and decide with data.

The issues of the project management have been interested in the structure, discipline and execution. Waterfall, agile, SCRUM, and hybrid frameworks have known techniques to plan the work, risk management and value delivery. Most of these frameworks were however formulated at a time when data was minimal, slow and in most cases retroactive. The current data is non-discrete, real-time, and is established in all business processes. The project management methodologies are vulnerable to turn into rigid checklists instead of being adaptive when they do not have analytics attached to them. This book examines the value of analytics in changing project management as a reactive practice into a strategic, proactive, predictive practice.

Fundamentally, this book deals with translation. It is commonly viewed as a technical or abstract and specialized field of data analytics. In contrast, project managers are supposed to coordinate people, processes and priorities, often without time or training to decipher complicated analytical models. Data Meets Decisions fills this gap between these two worlds. It breaks down the ideas of analysis and translates them into the language of a project and reforms data not as something that is scary and technical, but as a decision-making tool that makes judgment, clarity, and confidence better.

Instead of basing this book on theory alone, the book is based on real life stories which are based on different industries and positions. Reading about professionals like Sarah, Tom, Emma, and others, the readers observe the problems they may encounter at work: disorganized information, mismatched measurements, teams within a silo, lack of clarity of priorities and confusion in stress. Such stories are not imaginary digressions; they are educative vehicles. Both stories demonstrate how data-based thinking transforms discussions, eliminates ambiguity and achieves better results. We do not seek perfection, but progress--the elimination of guesswork, the replacement of assumptions by insight, of the opinions we have made.

One of the topics that are re-emerging in this book is non-technical data literacy. Data literacy does not presuppose writing a complex code or creating high-tech machine-learning models. It includes the ability to interpret what data is, posing the appropriate questions, identifying constraints and reporting findings. In the case of project managers this has evolved into a competency that is quickly becoming as important as scheduling, or risk management. Data-illiterate leaders may fail to interpret dashboards correctly, embrace problematic metrics, or make high-betterment decisions with partial information. On the other hand, developers who come up with even basic data mastery are credible, influence and strategic.

Another point that the book highlights is that analytics is not an isolated activity, it has to be integrated into the project processes. The value of analytics is only created when it informs the planning, execution, monitoring, and decision-making. The readers will get to know how the data is incorporated in project start up, project scope, stakeholder management, risk assessment, resource allocation, and performance monitoring. Since the difference between data lakes and data warehouses can be understood to the implementation of predictive and real-time analytics in agile environments, the theme is always the same: analytics must be an aid to the project and not a burden.

The discussion also revolves around ethics, governance and trust. The ethical burden to manage such data increases with the rise of projects that are more dependent on information about customers, employees and operations. There are no better ways to destroy trust or hurt results than to have poor data quality or hidden prejudice or poor governance. This book deals directly with these realities, highlighting transparency, accountability, and responsible data usage as the main elements of the current project leadership.

Data Meets Decisions has been written to project managers, program managers, product leaders, business analysts, and professionals that work at the nexus of execution and strategy. The concepts studied here can be widely extended, regardless of what you are in charge of be it software development, digital transformation, infrastructure, finance, or operations. Tools and illustrations cut across industries, however, the thinking is universal: improved data results in improved decisions, and improved decisions result in improved projects.

In sum, the book concludes that the future of project management is not determined by emerging methodologies, but the ability of leaders to utilize information to manage complexity. There is no replacement of experience or intuition by analytics, it only enhances these. The combination of data and human judgment makes the projects stronger, flexible and purposeful towards the organizational objectives.

Data is another aspect onto which you are presented as you continue to read the chapters that follow not as a noise, not as a technical burden, but as a strategic associate. The data to decision journey is not the preserve of experts, but of all project leaders who are ready to pose better questions and desire to find better answers. This book is your roadmap on that trip.

CHAPTER 01

INTRODUCTION TO DATA ANALYTICS AND PROJECT MANAGEMENT

...■...■...

Journey into Data-Driven Project Management

In the bustling corridors of a mid-sized technology company in Silicon Valley, Sarah Thompson, a certified Project Management Professional (PMP), was diligently juggling the day-to-day challenges of managing multiple projects. With over a decade of experience, Sarah was a seasoned project manager who had mastered the art of managing teams, timelines, and deliverables. Yet, on this Monday morning in early 2023, she was left looking at a chaotic spreadsheet that was the end result of weeks of work. The data was distributed-across the organization, in separate compartments, sales data from one department, customer reviews from another, operational data buried in email. Her team was guessing and building on imprecise data, resulting in hold-ups, cost overruns and unsatisfied stakeholders.

Sarah's project was to launch a new software product that was designed to improve user engagement for their clients. Our goal was clear at the beginning: 6 months, a cross-function team of developers, marketers and analysts, and firmer check points. However, as the weeks went by, discrepancies did arise. While the marketing team were unanimous it was popular, based on anecdotal surveys by the users, the development team were concerned about bottlenecking in the backend infrastructure. And with no single source of truth across the organization, efforts to resolve these discrepancies became like plowing through a foggy night for Sarah's company. Meetings dragged on, discussions were opinion and evidence driven. "I think what customers really want is feature X," one member of the team said, only to be shot down by another hunch.

It was while reviewing for finals late one night that Sarah had her epiphany. Browsing her tablet, she came across an article in her industry that described a case study of a similar firm that had incorporated data analytics into the way they managed projects. The results were nothing less than revolutionary: 40% reduction in decision-making time, better allocation of resources and project success rates improved by an astonishing 25%. Sarah became interested and started to ask questions. She understood that data analytics wasn't just for data scientists; it was a tool that project managers like her could use to filter through the noise, to find patterns, to use data-driven decisions that made sense in the context of strategic objectives.

So the next day, Sarah proposed to her team a small experiment. Others would take the information from several sources to create a center of control using simple analytics platforms. There was initial reluctance from non-technical members who thought it might make their working lives more difficult. One marketer said he was not a coder. But Sarah reassured them: "This is empowerment and not expertise." We'll start simple." As they continued to visualize trends in real-time - capturing correlation between customer feedback and feature usage, for example - the light came on. For them, all of their choices took data as an evidence basis:

they gave high priority to data-supported features, actively and quickly updated their timelines and included stakeholders with compelling visuals.

By the conclusion of the project, not only was the software deployed on time and under budget, but the rate of user adoption was 15% higher than expectations. Sarah's story is not unique - hers is a tale as old as time for countless project managers struggling with the information overload of the new millennium. Here we will establish the meeting point between data analytics and project management, and explain how those like Sarah can use data to drive efficiency, innovation, and success. We then see how, through a sequence of stories, mixing analytical insights with the traditional project disciplines can be transformative, which leads into the practical recommendations to come.

Overview of Data Analytics and Its Role in Project Management

Data analytics is the systematic computational analysis of data to extract data, patterns, correlations and knowledge that can be used for making decisions. It covers a range of techniques ranging from descriptive analytics (what actually occurred), to diagnostic (why it occurred), to predictive (what could occur) and prescriptive (what should be done). In the realm of project management, data analysis serves as a bridge between data and decisions, enabling managers to optimize processes, mitigate risks, and enhance outcomes.

Historically, project management was based on qualitative estimation, and judgment based on experience. Gantt Charts and Critical Path methods provided structure but the dynamism to deal with the complexities of modern day projects where data from IoT, cloud, and social media platform explosion is out of control. Enter data analytics: it makes this data deluge a strategic asset. For example, in a construction project, analytics can identify material shortages based on data across the supply chain or in software development, forecast sprint velocities based on past performance metrics for the development team.

Data analytics do more than just affect project management in one way. First, it is a more effective tool for risk management because it is designed to reveal possible problems before they occur. Through the use of statistical modeling, project managers can quantify risks (e.g., the likelihood that delays due to vendor unreliability will occur) and devise contingency plans. Second, it is better at allocating resources. By understanding workloads and productivity patterns, teams can better assign tasks to minimize burnout and maximize efficiency. Third, it leads to stakeholder engagement. Real-time dashboards: Visualization of progress through analytics-driven reports, such as heat maps or trend lines, build trust and enable buy-in better than static documents.

Examine how analytics are being built into portfolio management. Multi-project management: for the organizations that are handling several projects, analytics can help you prioritize projects according to the expected ROI in the context of business goals. A recent survey of business departments conducted by the Project Management Institute (PMI) indicates organizations with a high level of analytics maturity are 2.5 times more likely to finish a project on time and within budget. This is because analytics is a feedback loop: real-time data monitoring enables agile adjustments where potential failures can be used for optimization.

Also, data analytics makes information democratic. Data silos are the traditional playing field for analytics: silos fill statistical gaps by unifying commonly used data. For project managers this means a change from reactive leadership to proactive. Instead of waiting for firewalls to fail, they predict them In Sarah's case, analytics found that correlations existed between spikes in customer feedback and specific feature deployments, enabling her team to iterate much more quickly.

A key component of this integration is understanding the nature of the data to be created: structured (e.g. databases) versus unstructured (e.g. e-mail) and ensuring that data quality is maintained through cleaning and validation processes. Ethical considerations are also important - analytics need to comply with legislation like the GDPR, they also help keep data private and help reduce bias. In the end, data analytics lets project managers go beyond their gut emotions to offer a firm basis for good strategy, one that can support sustainable achievement.

The Importance of Data Literacy for Non-Technical Professionals

Data literacy-the ability to read, understand, create and communicate data as information-is no longer an esoteric skill offered only to analysts or IT specialists. For non-technical project management staff, it's a necessary skill that forms the link between data geeks and decision-makers. In an era where data drives business deliberation and operations, project managers who are not data-worthy are in danger of being marginalized and harming their abilities to freely use information that generates competitive advantage.

Why is data literacy crucial? Above all, it enables better decision making. In contrast, non-technical professionals may have access to data reports, dashboards, or meetings but, if they lack data literacy, they can easily misinterpret data or fail to recognize nuance. For instance, knowing the difference between correlation and causation helps avoid drawing the wrong conclusions, such as believing marketing is responsible for a sales drop when an outside factor like a poor economy is causing the drop. Data literacy provides project managers with the opportunity to ask the right questions: "What does this metric actually represent?" Or what is:

How valid is this dataset?

In addition, it fosters inter-disciplinary work. Data literacy in multidisciplinary teams leads to shared language. An agile project manager who understands the basics of analytics can serve as a bridge between the rank and file programmers crunching code and the executive managers who want summary information. This eliminates communication gaps and speeds up project cycles Sarah, who at first felt overwhelmed by data, defined herself through self-study, beginning with the relatively simple notions, mean versus median, that helped her to accurately interpret data on team performance.

Data Literacy is a multi-stage process of building capabilities. Basic knowledge of the key concepts: types of data (quantitative vs. qualitative data), basic statistics (averages, variance), visualization rules (choose graphics representation that avoids distortion). Massive open online courses from sites and this easy for anyone, even without coding experience. Second, used as an analysis tool: run through sample datasets to derive insights (for example, projection of trends for project timelines).

For non-technical jobs data literacy also stresses ethical and critical thinking. Surveyors should be sensitive to factors that may bias data collection (e.g., surveys that are not representative of all possible demographics) and support inclusive methods. In project management terms, this means more equitable resource allocation and more equitable results.

Organizations can help in this regard by introducing training programs. Capacity building workshops in areas like Excel for basic analytics or Google Data Studio for visualization enable teams to take charge. The winning for organizations is high: Gartner shows that data-driven organizations will increase their efficiency by 20% more than the competition in customer satisfaction and increase their operational efficiency by 20%. Project manager Sarah became a data literate project leader, moving from coordinator to strategic leader who could link her projects back to data-informed outcomes.

In essence, data literacy democratizes analytics so non-technical professionals can stop being passive consumers and become active creators in the data ecosystem. It cultivates thinking skills with curiosity and skepticism serving to inform the processing of information and ultimately build project resilience and innovation.

Transforming from passive observation into active engagement with data alters the way that non-technical professionals approach challenges. They base their strategies on both intuition and anecdotes, but also empirical knowledge. This evolution doesn't diminish the importance of experience and intuition; it enhances them by grounding decisions on measurable trends. For project managers the schedules, budgets, and resources are no longer taken by a hunch but based on past performance metrics and predictive indicators. People who think with data are able to figure out what will take place, make changes and stay on course and communicate with assurance when things don't go as planned.

A proper understanding and interpretation of data within the story of a project enhances foresight. Those who can interpret leading indicators (such as early changes in customer behavior, supply chain performance or team productivity) can identify potential disruptions before they get out of hand. This proactive view decreases the amount of firefighting that is eating up team time. Over time, it becomes credible as stakeholders witness the individual managing the ambiguity with facts rather than speculation.

Data literacy develops a culture of accountability. When every member of the team is aware of the way the results are measured, performance is no longer subjective. Progress: it becomes a collective responsibility and not solely a manager's decision. In general, non-technical people who can explain the impact of their work on key metrics make it easier to achieve transparency and collective ownership. This clarity dissolves silos between technical specialists and operational staff, providing a fluid environment in which everyone is assured of goals and the evidence on which decisions are based.

Data literacy also enhances communication with top management. Executives and sponsors prefer brief reports that are results-oriented. A project manager that can tell a compelling story based on their complex data sets can speak the language and translate raw data into powerful business cases. In other words, instead of individual numbers, they put data in the context of organizational objectives, market dynamics, and risk analysis. This skill enhances their leverage in decision making forums as not just implementers of directions, but trusted advisors.

As companies adopt digital transformation, the volume of data and the variety continue to increase exponentially. This expansion is one of opportunity and challenge. Literacy is a prerequisite for abundance, which means there is the potential for information overload, with critical information being lost in the noise. Data literate professionals identify the metrics that signal what really matters, remove the noise of irrelevant metrics and pay attention to the metrics that directly affect project outcomes. This approach ensures that teams are working together and no effort is wasted on improving numbers that do not drive value.

Data literacy boosts the risk management capabilities. Every project is subject to uncertainty, but data can be used to quantify and prioritize risks. Risk models that support contingency plans can be developed by non-technical personnel familiar with notions such as probability distributions, variance, trend analysis, and so on. Rather than responding to crises, they will be able to head them off by noticing warning patterns in advance. This safeguards resources and develops resilience - projects are rebuilt more quickly when driven by informed foresight rather than reactive response.

An equally important aspect of data literacy is its ethical aspect. With ever more data-that is, information about individuals (like customer demographics, employee performance or stakeholder feedback)-in the hands of professionals, it is more important than ever to ensure privacy and fair behavior. Literacy includes having an understanding of the rules of governance of data, compliance requirements, and how biased data can impact society. A project manager who understands such ethical discussion points can advocate for responsible data practices to ensure that decisions are made by keeping legal standards and respect for human dignity in mind. This stewardship leads to trust, which is the key to long term success.

Ideally, data literacy is not a one-time competency, but should be considered as part of a continuous learning process. Data landscape changes rapidly: new visualization tools emerge, new analytic methods become better and regulations are changed. The only way to keep up is to learn all the time via formal training or informal interactions with colleagues. Mentorships, cross-department collaboration and communities of practice accelerate this growth, allowing the non-technical staff to learn from specialists while providing operational insight. The reciprocal transaction has a positive impact for both parties and generates shared meaning.

Companies that understand the cost of not having data-literate workers tend to reap serious benefits in terms of efficiency, innovation, and agility. When experimentation is safer and smarter, it is safer because employees at every level can work with data. Teams can test new approaches, make evidence-informed decisions and iterate quickly. This type of feedback loop generates innovation, as ideas are challenged hard rather than being cast aside because of doubt. It also decreases resistance to change, as the data literate teams can see the tangible benefits of change rather than making it an abstract mandate.

For individuals, data literacy can help them advance in their careers. Companies need people who are able to cross boundaries - between technical and business functions or between change initiatives and strategy. Their ability to draw different inputs into meaningful recommendations distinguishes them in competitive environments. This evolution from executor to strategist is an extension of the entire industry, where the key to success is now leading initiatives with insight and foresight rather than simply "getting stuff done."

Ultimately, data literacy helps non-technical professionals compete in a world that is data rich but data literate poor. It helps to turn raw numbers into meaningful knowledge, makes actions equal to results and raises the level of ordinary work to strategic contributions. As organisations become more complex, people with this competency will continue to make a difference and ensure progress - to ensure a future with well-informed and evidence-based decision making, and where all professionals, technical or otherwise, can lead with clarity and confidence.

Integrating Project Management Methodologies with Analytics: Initialization and Tools

Data analytics brings intelligence to project management, and project management methodologies provide the frameworks for getting things done. This section discusses how methodologies such as Agile, SCRUM, and Waterfall can be combined with analytics, including how to begin a data-driven project and how to make good use of the tools.

This incremental process works very well with analytics. In Agile, sprints are for planning, doing, and reviewing; analytics improves each stage by providing a chance to deliver feedback in real-time. For example, predictive analytics for burndown charts can help predict utilization to enable teams to dynamically adjust backlogs. A version of Agile, SCRUM (Scrum) helps with analytics for the daily stand-up and retrospectives. Remember, velocity is just one of the metrics that data tools can collect to improve processes, including specific bottlenecks that may be identified as recurring delays in various testing phases.

However, Waterfall is more of a linear structure that relies on upfront planning, and analytics lends itself exceptionally well to requirements gathering. Predictive modeling can simulate project outcomes based on past data and therefore limit uncertainties for the future stages. Hybrid models, which combine elements of Waterfall and Agile, use analytics to make decisions on when to switch, such as to an iterative development model if data suggests a high volatility.

An important first step for a data-driven project is to clearly identify its goals. Use SMART (Specific, Measurable, Achievable, Relevant, Time-bound) criteria based on data baselines For Sarah's project, to get a 20% increase in adoption via the product, they set targets through analysing how the product had performed in previous launches. Next, identify stakeholders; which can be achieved through mapping using analytics to determine their level of influence and interest (and prioritizing engagement based on data such as past involvement metrics).

Clear KPIs - Define key performance indicators such as on-time delivery rate or ROI that can be measured using data sources. Tools make this possible: project management solutions like Trello (for visual boards) or Jira (for issue tracking) are integrated with analytics solutions like Power BI or Tableau. Power BI offers the drag-and-drop creation of visualizations (by adding them to a blank canvas), and Tableau is perfect for creating interactive dashboards from complex datasets.

Practical steps include Data Collection Planning: Sources are defined, ensured to integrate (e.g. via APIs) and governed for quality Then, develop an analytical track: from descriptive analytics for baseline information, then to predictive, which is forecasting.

Basic principles are the foundation for this integration: assumption is replaced by evidence (data-driven decision-making); an analytical mindset is based on hypothesis-testing; alignment is a key principle to ensure that analytics are supporting the project and not the reverse. In the case of Sarah's transformation, these things came together to bring scattered data into a unified strategy.

Integration of analytics into processes and tools enables project managers to build robust systems that are adaptable to change, value adding, and continuous improvement. This approach drives projects toward success in a data-driven world.

The confluence of project management methods and analytics is also the transition from blindly completing tasks to being evidence driven in their coordination. When analytics is embedded in projects, it no longer has a support role but is actually a strategic partner. The difference between Agile, SCRUM and Waterfall becomes dynamic ecosystems where every decision is always being driven by quantifiable data. This change is particularly effective at the project start when the early decisions establish the conditions for future outcomes.

Project initiation is often where the success or failure of the project is made before ever starting it. Traditional practices are focused on scope definition, approvals, and drafting charters. Analytics adds a level of precision which strengthens each step. When goals are prosed, historical data can be used to validate the feasibility of the goals. For example, if a company has an average time of ten months to deliver an enterprise software and a new project promises six months, analytics helps to reveal the discrepancy between the ambitions and reality. This initial revelation means that the discrepancy between desire and what is feasible is avoided.

Stakeholder analysis is also benefited from analytics. Mapping influence networks no longer uses organizational charts. Social-network tools identify the patterns of collaboration, frequency of communication and influence on decisions in the digital workspaces. Project managers can identify formal stakeholders as well as informal influencers who can accelerate or derail progress. Engagement plans move from static plans to models that are dynamic based on the data of sentiment, responsiveness, and behavior.

Risk assessment, which was a qualitative exercise up until now, becomes quantitatively based. Machine learning models that have been trained from past projects can predict that a project will be over budget, that there will be schedule slippages or quality problems, based on pre-indicators such as the complexity of requirements, the composition of the team or the reliability of the vendors. "These predictions can enable teams to develop contingency buffers to the actual level of risk instead of using arbitrary allowances." This analytical rigour transforms the phase of initiation from a subjective planning phase to a statistically informed launch pad.

In agile environments, analytics is a turbo charger in terms of feedback. Iterative cycles mean huge data flows - velocity charts, sprint burndowns, defect logs, story point completions - which analytics synthesizes into understandable signals. Therefore, regression models can be used to supply not only reporting but also causal inference about sprint characteristics and outcomes. For example, analytics might indicate that cross-functional teams that are evenly distributed with experienced and junior developers have a consistently higher performance than others, and that means that resource allocation will be adjusted accordingly in future sprints.

Sentiment analysis can also be used to enhance retrospectives. By looking at the communication from collaboration tools, leaders can identify subtle changes in morale that may not be detected in meetings. These insights are used to take targeted actions - share the load or clarify requirements - before productivity is affected by drop-off. Anomaly detection algorithms can identify deviations in sprint patterns at an early stage, allowing for proactive corrections rather than reactive fixes.

Agile ceremonies are more effective if they are supported by real-time dashboards. Jira connected to Power BI or Tableau can be used to display live visualizations of backlog health, throughput trends, and cycle times when sprint planning is occurring. This transparency supports data-driven discussions instead of subjective debates and enables teams to self-organize around evidence instead of hierarchy. This results in an Agile environment in which analytics manages to strengthen agility by bringing unambiguous insights that are actionable at each iteration.

In Waterfall projects where phases follow in sequence, analytics ensures greater planning and monitoring. Scope definition becomes better with the use of parametric estimation models where historical data from similar projects is used to predict effort and cost. During the design phase, simulation tools are used to model the interdependencies among the various tasks and discover critical path sensitivities and the possibility of testing scenarios before they are actually executed.

The ability to offer fine grained control is provided by the earned-value management (EVM) metrics as well as real-time data feeds that are generated during the execution process. Automated EVM dashboards constantly update cost & schedule performance, immediately alerting on deviation. Predictive models then project final costs and completion dates based on current trends - which provides leadership early alerts beyond the point of partial completion that traditional milestone reviews cannot.

Analytics-based defect prediction can also be used to improve quality assurance. By analyzing code complexity, developer history and change frequency of modules, predictive algorithms determine which modules are at high risk of causing defects in testing. Allocating additional reviews or automated tests to these hotspots minimizes rework and ensures delivery on time. Thus, analytics helps to bring back the agility to the otherwise rigid Waterfall model, while retaining its disciplined structure.

Many organizations are now moving towards hybrid approaches that blend the flexibility of Agile and the predictability of Waterfall. In these environments, analytics is the strand which binds everything together. Data-driven readiness assessments are used to clarify transition points including changes from a structured planning phase to iterative development. Requirements volatility, resource utilization rates, indices of market condition are metrics that indicate when a project needs to be moved from fixed plans to adaptive cycles.

Portfolio-level analytics only adds to hybrid governance. By pooling metrics from projects that use different methodologies, leaders are able to see which methodology delivers the highest ROI in certain scenarios. Over time, this evidence base helps to contribute to the choice of methodology itself, transforming what had originally been a philosophical debate into one made on the basis of data. The hybrid environment transforms into a living laboratory where data works on optimizing processes as well as outcomes continuously.

The melding of methodologies and analytics increases the arsenal available to the project manager. Tools are no longer chosen to be able to schedule or manage tasks; they are chosen to be able to generate and interpret data. Trello, for example, provides some integrations that convert card movement patterns into flow efficiency charts. Jira API provides rich activity information that can be used in advanced modeling custom pipelines.

For further analysis, tools like Tableau and Power BI can provide interactive dashboards that can draw from different sources like financial systems, time tracking tools, bug tracking systems, etc. into consolidated project performance views. Suppose you have a Microsoft Project file and you want to predict the probability of slippage for each task based on the historical data, Microsoft Project may be enhanced with predictive plugins that can do just that. Documentation using a collaborative workspace such as Notion or Confluence can display live analytics panels inside the documentation so that insights are available in daily workflows.

Emerging AI-driven platforms go beyond that, however, to provide prescriptive analytics. Not only do these systems predict what will happen, they also recommend courses of action, such as moving resources from one workstream to another to prevent a delay from happening, or even to prevent a potential delay. Natural language processing can be used to analyze project communications to identify gaps between stated objectives and actual project activities. As these tools become more mature, the role of project manager turns from that of a data collector to a strategic interpreter, with the role evolving into a role of taking that data generated by machines and turning it into actionable insights.

This integration cannot be maintained by technology alone; attitude is also important. Infusing analytics into the methodology involves teams' approaches to data as a common language rather than an area of specialization. This culture transformation begins by demystifying analytics - equipping members to read basic metrics, question assumptions, and have evidence-based conversations. Sprint reviews can be supplemented with short analytics debriefs that provide the ability to see how metrics relates to results so that literacy is increased incrementally without overloading people with its details.

Another pillar is that of stimulating curiosity. Teams should be allowed to build hypotheses, such as "Increasing throughput by reducing review cycle time" and then test them against project data. This practice is scientific: experiments are small, controlled and objectively assessed. Over time, these habits form a self-correcting environment where decisions are confirmed or refined by evidence instead of ingrained habits.

Clergymen and priests have a particularly important role to play. When managers are explicit about the data they are using in their decision-making, why they have chosen specific metrics, and when results do not match expectations, they normalize analytical transparency. This creates psychological safety, where other people are encouraged to work with data without worrying about revealing errors. As the members of the team develop their ability to interpret patterns, anticipate risks and find opportunities together, the team's intelligence grows.

As analytics becomes embedded into methodologies, governance should develop as well. Reliable data is essential for evidence-based decision making; the lack of reliable data weakens the foundation of evidence-based decision making. Creating clear roles of data steward ensures that sources are validated, definitions are standardized and privacy rules are maintained. This is particularly important when dealing with projects that are personal or sensitive, as data breaches can result in legal and reputational harm.

Bias mitigation is also very important. Algorithms that are trained on skewed historical data can perpetuate inequities for example, underestimating the time that needs to be spent on complex initiatives if it was rushed on past projects. Regular bias audits - modeling assumptions, training datasets, and output patterns - help to maintain fairness. The inclusion of different points of view in review processes can help to recognize blind spots that are not always identified by pure technical inspections. This ethical vigilance ensures compliance and fosters stakeholder trust.

Furthermore, transparency is an important pillar of governance. Transparency in analytic techniques - publishing how predictions are created, what variables have the highest weighted values, and what assumptions and constraints are present - will help to create confidence in their application. Stakeholders have a higher chance of accepting data-driven suggestions if they have a clear grasp of where suggestions come from. Openness is a defense against the black box conception that would make adoption difficult, particularly in non-technical participants.

As more and more projects incorporate analytics, organizations can evaluate their maturity profile along this dimension. Maturity models assess the capabilities along several axes: data availability, tool adoption, analytical capabilities, decision practices and culture. Early-stage teams may be using manual reports and simple metrics, whereas more advanced teams are implementing real-time dashboards, predictive models, and automated decision-aid.

Continual maturity assessments show progress and gaps and drive targeted investments. For example, a team with sophisticated tools but low analytical literacy might focus on training while a team with good analysts but poor data integration infrastructure might focus on integration infrastructure. This iterative development means that analytics integration is ever-changing as the business grows and not one that stagnates following initial implementation.

Continuous improvement is based on feedback loops. Learning from projects - good and bad - about how analytics affected project outcomes makes it possible to refine methodologies. Over time, this creates an institutional knowledge base of best practices, benchmarks and validated metrics that speed progress of future initiatives. The development organization becomes more and more adaptive, capable of implementing complex projects with speed and accuracy.

Ultimately, when project management methodologies are blended with analytics, not only do individual projects run more efficiently, but the capability of the organization changes. Projects cease being isolated efforts, but rather become nodes of data in strategic network. Input from one project builds on the next to create a heterogeneous effect, wherein each implementation increases the intelligence of the enterprise as a whole.

CHAPTER 02

GATHERING SCATTERED DATA: THE FOUNDATION OF ANALYTICS

The Reality of Scattered Data in Modern Projects

A. Story Introduction: Tom's Challenge

Tom had been managing the projects almost ten years, and he believed that he experienced all the possible issues: deadlines, priorities, reduced budgets. Not even an attempt to find the answer to a very simple question posed by one of the executives helped him: What is the current status of the project?

Scattered about he had fragments of the answer. Status updates were lost in lengthy email attentions. The budget figures existed in a dashboard of Oracle NetSuite available to the finance department only. The Sales forecasts were kept within Salesforce, and the development backlog was kept within Jira. Meanwhile, one of the operations people had his own spreadsheet, which had been going against everything at this point.

Tom took hours to copy, paste and reconcile these pieces in order to create a report. Towards the end of his work, the information became obsolete. The experience made him wonder how any decisions could be made decisively when the basis of it data was so disintegrated.

His struggle is not unique. This is the same concern of many project managers: all the crucial information is there, but it is like puzzle pieces that were scattered across the various rooms. Without uniting those pieces, any analysis is doomed to fail in the first place.

B. Common Types of Data Sources

To solve the problem of scattered data, we first need to understand where it lives. Project data today flows through a complex digital ecosystem, often divided into structured, semi-structured, and unstructured sources.

1. **Structured Data Sources**
   Structured data lives in defined fields and tables. It is easy to query and analyze but often resides in siloed platforms:

- **Customer Relationship Management (CRM)** systems like Salesforce and HubSpot hold customer data, sales pipelines, and deal histories.
- **Enterprise Resource Planning (ERP)** platforms such as SAP and Oracle NetSuite contain financials, procurement, and supply chain information.
- **Relational Databases** like PostgreSQL or MySQL house operational and transactional records.

2. **Semi-Structured Data Sources**

These systems hold data in loosely organized formats, often requiring extra effort to normalize:

- **APIs (Application Programming Interfaces)** — internal or external REST APIs streaming JSON data.
- **Project management tools** such as Jira, Trello, or Asana producing activity logs and task histories.
- **Cloud storage platforms** like Google Drive and Microsoft OneDrive, where structured spreadsheets and free-form documents coexist.

3. **Unstructured Data Sources**
Some of the most critical project signals are locked in free text or media files:

- Emails and chat threads with requirements, clarifications, and approvals.
- Meeting recordings or transcripts.
- Notes from field teams or customer support logs.
- Sensor and device feeds from IoT devices, often arriving as raw time-series data.

Each of these sources contains valuable insights. Yet because they live in different formats and systems, they resist easy combination.

C. Challenges Created by Scattered Data

When data is scattered, project managers face invisible friction every day.

1. **Data Silos**
Different teams own different systems, creating barriers. Marketing controls the CRM, finance owns

the ERP, and engineering lives in their issue tracker. No one has a full picture.

2. **Version Chaos**
   Spreadsheets circulate through emails with conflicting numbers. By the time data is presented in a meeting, three new versions have emerged.
3. **Loss of Metadata**
   Raw figures often arrive without context—no timestamp, author, or source trail—making it impossible to verify accuracy.
4. **Format Inconsistencies**
   Dates written as MM/DD/YYYY in one file and DD/MM/YYYY in another. Currency columns mixed with text. These mismatches cause errors in analysis.
5. **Limited Visibility for Leaders**
   Executives must rely on slow, manual reporting cycles. They make strategic decisions based on stale snapshots rather than real-time insight.
6. **Security and Compliance Risks**
   When data lives in uncontrolled locations like personal drives or private inboxes, it becomes vulnerable to breaches, leaks, or violations of data privacy regulations like GDPR or CCPA.

These challenges are not just technical inconveniences—they carry real business costs. Delayed insights lead to delayed actions, which can derail project schedules and inflate budgets.

D. Strategic Implications

Sporadic information does not merely complicate the life but it actually defeats the objective of analytics. Analytics requires good clean, full and contextual data to give meaningful results. When data is fragmented:

• Projected forecasts are not accurate and thus resulting into inaccurate resource planning.

• KPIs lose credibility and it becomes hard to gain a measure of progress.

• The teams waste time on reconciling numbers than on enhancing results.

This is the reason why the process of data consolidation is not some optional activity but some form of strategic prerequisite. It is the initial level of maturity of any project management structure that uses analytics. Predictive modeling, advanced dashboards, or AI tools are pouring sand on the beach until the data is unified.

In the case of Tom, the realization of this changed his attitude; collecting data was not an ancillary activity, but rather it was included in the critical path as part of the project. His initial step was the development of a single point of data one source of truth that all stakeholders would rely on. It is only at this point that sophisticated analytics are able to unlock the value.

II. Designing a Data Consolidation Strategy

A. Framing Data Consolidation as a Project Objective

The pioneer move that Tom made was the ability to no longer see data collection as a by-product but then begin to approach it the same way any other deliverable. He created a specific workstream of Data Foundation within his project plan with its owners and deadlines and quality standards.

He created a stepwise roadmap instead of attempting to clean everything simultaneously:

1. Discovery Phase- Listing all available sources of data used by both teams.

2. Consolidation Phase- Designing how these sources would be fed into a central repository.

3. Validation Phase - Checking the assembled data on its accuracy, freshness and completeness.

4. Maintenance Phase- Developing processes of continuous updates and governance.

When Tom put this roadmap on the critical path of the project, he re-positioned data gathering as strategic infrastructure. This change of mind-set is necessary. There are no clear ownerships and milestones, which causes the collapse of data consolidation efforts under their own weight.

In order to control the expectations, he applied common project management tools such as Microsoft Project and Jira to develop tasks, sprints, and dependencies. Each activity had its success criteria, like CRM data synchronized nightly into the central store or 95 percent of the fields are filled without any empty values.

B. Establishing Governance and Data Ownership

The failure of consolidation is usually caused by an ambiguous ownership. The various departments tend to leave the question of data quality to another individual and no one is held responsible. Tom dealt with this by constituting a data governance group, which was a small cross functional team representing the main data sources.

This group defined:

Data Owners This refers to individuals who hold responsibility to ensure accuracy and timeliness of particular sources (such as the Salesforce sales operations manager to Salesforce data).

Data Stewards are also personnel in charge of ensuring data quality, cleansing mistakes, and updating data.

• Access Policies - Who was allowed to access, edit or export data in each system subject to such principles as least privilege.

• Security and Compliance Protocols — Making certain compliance with such frameworks as GDPR and CCPA, in particular with personal data.

He recorded these in a chart of Data Charter that was endorsed officially by the project sponsors. This made the effort legitimate and avenues of escalation in case of disputes.

The outcome was a cultural, not a technical, one the teams started to see data as an organizational possession and not as an individual property.

C. Mapping and Cataloging Data Sources

Governance brought Tom and his team to develop a data catalog, a list of all datasets they had intended to use. This catalog responded to three critical queries of each source:

1. What is it?

o Example: Salesforce Opportunities Table - organized records of sale deals, with close dates, amounts and owners.

2. Where is it?

o Location and system (cloud platform, local database, file share).

3. The structure and updating of how is it organized?

o Schema, data types, frequency of update, and volume of data.

They opened an account with Google Sheets to start with the catalog and subsequently transferred to the Data Catalog part of Microsoft Power BI to have dynamic updates of the catalog.

The development of this catalog uncovered unsuspected complexities of customers with different IDs in different systems, inconsistent product naming, and unknown legacy spreadsheets that continued to shape decision-making. This openness had enabled Tom to establish realistic cleanup as well as normalization plans prior to commencing integration.

D. Choosing a Consolidation Architecture

After mapping the data, Tom had to make a decision on the technical method of consolidating it. It has three primary architectural models that have trade-offs:

1. Centralized Data Warehouse

• All the information is duplicated to a single storage system such as Snowflake, Amazon Redshift or Google big query.

• Is comprised of consistent schema and mighty analytics, but with upfront effort on ETL (Extract, Transform, Load).

• Optimal where there is complicated cross-source analysis necessary.

2. Data Lake

• Stores raw, unstructured, and structured data in the same place, usually in a system such as Azure Data Lake or Amazon S3.

• Elastic with large, varied data sets but needs strong governance to prevent the loss of a data swamp.

3. Federated or Virtualized Layer.

• Stores the data of original systems, but forms virtual layer to query the data together with such tools as Denodo or Dremio.

• Easier to execute, however, requires well-established availability of source systems.

Tom chose a compromise strategy: transactional data was moved to a central warehouse every night, and volatile operational logs were called upon a federated layer to eliminate duplication. It was a balance that provided stability and freshness.

E. Defining Data Quality Standards

It is pointless to consolidate without quality. The governance group that Tom was a part of stipulated the following clear data quality dimensions to measure all incoming data:

• Completeness -Have obligatory fields been filled?

• Consistency -Are there consistent values across systems? (e.g. one list of countries)

• Accuracy - Are the values accurate (spot checks against source records)

• Timeliness - What is the freshness of the received data?

• Uniqueness -Are duplicate records being consolidated appropriately?

They established automated validation codes in Python and SQL queries to indicate anomalies. A simple example.

III. Tools and Techniques for Data Consolidation

In the event that organizations deal with disjointed information, the selection of the tools and methodology becomes central in sorting out and harmonizing information into one, easy to access format. In the case of Tom, summarizing email, spreadsheet and Salesforce data was a very important move. Automation and strategic planning were needed in the process. In this part we will discuss the most crucial tools, their functions in data consolidation, and a real-life example of a Python script.

A. Automation Tools to Move Data Smoothly.

Zapier is considered to be one of the most popular automation platforms that can be used to bridge gaps between different systems. It enables the user to make applications that are not usually related to each other communicate. As an example, Gmail data (or Outlook) may be directed to Google Sheets, or Salesforce data may be driven to a database.

The benefits of automation tools are:

- Lessen the use of manual errors through eradication of duplicated data input.
- Make sure that there is a real-time synchronization across various sources.
- Give the non-technical personnel the opportunity to make workflows without coding skills.

Zapier enabled Tom to create a system that would automatically trigger the customer inquiry email into a common spreadsheet, which would save time on responding to the customer question. This automation was the foundation of his original data pipeline.

B. Aggregation of Data using Cloud Spreadsheets.

Whereas automation tools pass data, platforms such as Google Sheets or Microsoft Excel serve as early staging platforms. The tools are free of charge, team-based, and they need less configuration.

Google Sheets served as an interim center of the team of Tom, which was collecting data of several departments, including sales, marketing and support, and then it was incorporated into the primary system. This enabled the stakeholders to access all the records at a single point even prior to database formal integration.

Best practices of using spreadsheet to do aggregation:

• Normalize column names and format of all sheets.

• Prevent errors when entering data by use of data validation rules.

• Secure important ranges in order to avoid any accidental overwrites.

• Adopt access controls in order to keep data safe.

C. SQL Connectors and Database.

The spreadsheets are inadequate as volumes of data increase. Here is where SQL connectors, and centralized databases come in. SQL connectors allow you to fetch information in various systems such as Oracle NetSuite, SAP or Salesforce and put it into a structured relational database.

Tom at some point converted his project data to PostgreSQL database though he was using Google Sheets initially. This action permitted more complicated querying, version control, and enhanced security.

Key benefits:

• High level of filtering and analytics with the help of SQL queries.

• Role-based access control would lead to increased security.

• Capability to manipulate big data without the slowdown of performance.

D. API Pulling of Real Time Data.

The modern systems offer APIs (Application Programming Interfaces) that allow you to pull programmatically with data. When it comes to having the latest information without the manual input, APIs come in particularly useful.

The following is an example of a Python script that Tom applied to retrieve project data on a REST API and transform it into a pandas DataFrame to continue working with it:

IV. Project Management Perspective — Treating Data Collection as a Milestone

For Tom, data consolidation was not just a technical task — it was a strategic milestone that shaped the trajectory of his entire project. From a project management standpoint, treating data collection as a formal milestone ensures it gets the attention, resources, and accountability it deserves. Without clear milestones, data efforts can easily become disorganized side-tasks instead of structured achievements that support decision-making.

This section will explore how project managers can plan, execute, and track data collection as a key deliverable.

A. Defining Data Collection Objectives in the Project Plan

Data collection should be approached like any other project deliverable: with clear goals, scope, and success criteria.

Steps Tom followed:

1. **Objective Setting:** He defined what questions the unified dataset needed to answer, such as customer engagement trends and project timelines.
2. **Scope Definition:** He documented all sources of data to be consolidated: Salesforce CRM records, support emails, and shared spreadsheets.
3. **Stakeholder Alignment:** He gained buy-in from department heads who owned various data sources, ensuring cooperation.

Key project planning tip: Include a "Data Readiness" deliverable in your project charter, with expected inputs, responsible owners, and approval criteria. This gives it the same weight as development or design milestones.

B. Assigning Roles and Responsibilities

Clear ownership avoids confusion. In Tom's case, scattered data belonged to multiple teams, which initially created bottlenecks. He created a responsibility matrix (RACI model) for data collection activities:

Task	Responsible	Accountable	Consulted	Informed
Gathering CRM records	Sales Analyst	Sales Manager	IT Administrator	Project Team

Extracting support emails	Operations Lead	Project Manager	Customer Support	Project Team
Cleaning and merging datasets	Data Analyst	Project Manager	All Departments	Executive Sponsor

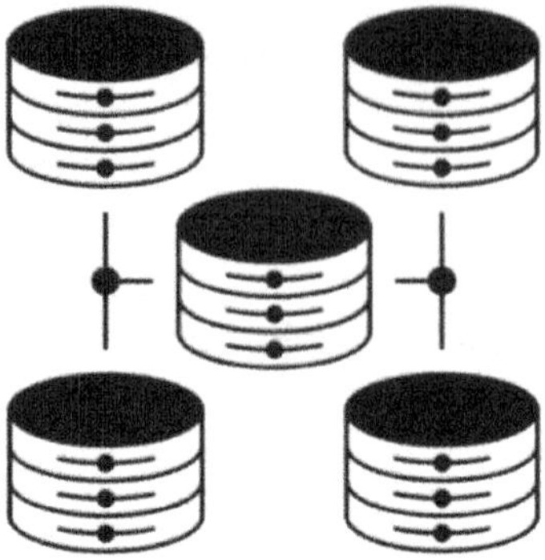

CHAPTER 3:

DATA LAKES VS. DATA WAREHOUSES: STRUCTURING YOUR DATA

The Story and Core Concepts

Emma Ruiz did not work as a data scientist. She was an effective project manager in a developing logistic company, balancing between contracting vendors, delivery schedules and unlimited project meetings. She was working with tasks and people rather than algorithms and storage structures. But in the spring of 2024, Emma was gazing at a drawing on a whiteboard in a conference room, which would ultimately transform her whole perception of how the data was driving the projects that she was in charge of.

Her company was growing at a very fast pace as it opened new warehouses in various regions and even installed IoT sensors into its delivery vans. The outcome was the blast of new information. All the trucks broadcasted telemetry on speed, temperature, and fuel economy. Every warehouse tracked package scanning, labor scheduling and operational throughput. In the meantime, the finance department had continued to use structured ERP reports in order to close the monthly and the customer service operated on CRM dashboards with tightly designed data fields.

The issue was that the company had no place to store all of this information in a sensible manner. Engineers were arguing in favour of a data lake which was a core storage point whereby all raw data could be thrown in and it could be examined later. The finance director desired a data warehouse- organized, tidy, and bi-optimized to generate business intelligence reports. Emma was approached by the CEO to arrange an assessment. She must have been quick a learner: what was the difference, and why did it matter?

Understanding the Core Difference

On the face of it, the words were synonymous. Both offered the ability to store data in the cloud, both indicated a promise of scaling, and both indicated that they supported analytics. However, Emma quickly found out that there is no distinction between data lakes and data warehouses any more basic than a library and a storage shed.

- Data Lake: A large repository where raw and unstructured data in their original form is stored, structured, semi-structured or unstructured. Imagine it is a huge vessel and there is nothing wasted. You do not have to worry about fitting sensor data, log files, emails, images or spreadsheets into predefined tables. A data lake is dynamic and forward-thinking: you do not know all the queries that you will require to ask, but you want to have the raw material on hand.

- Data Warehouse: A form of repository that is created to query, report and do analytics. A warehouse is an imposition, unlike the lake. Data is scrubbed, normalized and stored in performance optimized schema-defined tables. This is the place where business teams operate financial dashboards, sales trend analysis or KPI report. A data warehouse is data answer oriented- it is an arrangement of data in predictable formats that the executives can rely on.

Emma scribbled in her notebook:

"Lake = keep everything, structure later. Warehouse = clean and structure first."

Use Cases Through Emma's Lens

The examples of Emma on logistics projects provided textbook examples:

- IoT Sensor Data (Data Lake): Trucks were transmitting millions of rows of raw telemetry per week- temperature, GPS, fuel, vibration. These collections did not fit a rigid schema and the questions were all developing. What is the effect of driving on maintenance? Do temperature changes tell when it will spoil? A lake allows you to put it all out of your system and find patterns afterward.
- ERP Reports (Data Warehouse): ERP created by the finance team generated organized monthly costs, procurement, and inventory reports. These were standard, validated and audit ready. They needed accuracy and speed and not exploratory flexibility. A warehouse fit was a natural fit: a table by accounts,

cost center, and time period with which to present boards.

She started to observe the equilibrium: the two types of storage were appropriate to each other, depending on the nature of data and the requirements of the project.

The Broader Analogy: Kitchen vs. Pantry

Emma used a comparison to explain it to her technical-less-technical colleagues. “Imagine our data is like food.” She said. A data lake resembles a huge pantry in which we dump all of our purchases raw vegetables, tinned goods, half-opened sauces, frozen leftovers, etc. There it all is, but you have to sort it out when you are ready to cook. A data warehouse is a kitchen shelf containing only the basics, well labeled and divided up. Where sugar is required in the recipe you know exactly where to find it.

This metaphor resonated. A data Lake is rich and versatile, but may get disorganized. A data warehouse has consistency and organization although it requires greater preparation.

Technical Characteristics

Emma dug deeper into the technical distinctions, simplifying them for her project stakeholders:

1. **Data Types**
   - *Lake:* Stores everything—structured tables, semi-structured JSON logs, unstructured videos.
   - *Warehouse:* Primarily structured and sometimes semi-structured data.
2. **Schema**

- *Lake:* Schema-on-read (structure applied when analyzing).
- *Warehouse:* Schema-on-write (structure enforced when data is ingested).

3. **Processing**
   - *Lake:* ELT (Extract, Load, Transform)—data lands raw, transformed only when needed.
   - *Warehouse:* ETL (Extract, Transform, Load)—data is cleaned before entering.
4. **Cost and Scale**
   - *Lake:* Cheaper storage (e.g., AWS S3 charges per gigabyte stored).
   - *Warehouse:* More expensive but optimized for query performance.
5. **Users**
   - *Lake:* Data scientists, analysts exploring new questions.
   - *Warehouse:* Business users, executives relying on structured dashboards.

These distinctions helped Emma articulate why the company might need both, not just one.

When Project Managers Must Decide

In Emma, the moment had come when she understood that this is not just a technical discussion--it was project-management decision. Mismanagement might make her team go into a data swamp, a data lake that has no control but is filled with junk that cannot be used at all, or may spend months and over-engineer a warehouse that is suffocating creativity.

She re-packaged the question project wise:

- Scope definition: What do we need to know in business today as compared to tomorrow?
- Stakeholders: Who will get the data initially-finance with their harsh reporting requirements or engineering with their discovery modelling?
- Risk Management: What is the risk of holding excess raw data versus what is the risk of losing something good too soon?

This project attitude enabled her to close the divide between engineers, finance and leadership.

Story Interlude: The Meeting

During a single such meeting, the engineering team went on a tear in support of a lake. Their chief data scientist said that we do not know what models will we need in the future. We will lose a lot of context if we push ourselves into a warehouse form at this point. We should save all the raw data--all sensor pings, all log files.

The finance director was shaking his head. “That’s a recipe for chaos. We must have trustworthy figures, not a stack of statistics which none can believe. When we are reporting quarterly to auditors we can not base it on raw and messy logs.

The CEO turned to Emma. What is your suggestion then?

She took a breath. “Both. Let’s build a hybrid strategy. Lake to store our sensor data- cheap, flexible, future based. An ERP and financial data warehouse, organized, efficient, and conforming. They make a base on which we can develop.

The room quieted. It was the first time that the debate changed to both/and rather than either/or. The clarity of Emma had predetermined the realistic way forward..

Why This Matters for Project Managers

The story of Emma highlighted an important lesson: data storage does not rest solely in the hands of the IT-speakman: it is a component of the project. In defining deliverables, timelines and budgets, project managers have to enquire:

- Where will the data live?
- Who will access it, and how?
- Which trade-offs do we have between flexibility and reliability?

These questions cannot be ignored as the cause of delays, incorrect expectations, or even expensive rework. This is necessary since including them means that analytics work is based on the correct foundation.

Looking Ahead

Towards the end of her assessment, Emma had learned the data architecture language and was able to lead her crew. She did not have to write the necessary ETL pipeline codes or S3 bucket settings, yet she was aware of whom to ask the proper questions. She had mastered the necessary doctrine:

A data lake fuels discovery. Decisions are made by a data warehouse. They are the pillars of contemporary analytics.

Tools, Processes, and Applications in Project Management

The sketch made on the whiteboard by Emma gave the final resolution to the debate, but she was just starting her career as a project coordinator. It is not hard to explain that data lakes and warehouses play different roles; but getting the appropriate tools and processes in place and maintaining schedules and budgets is a whole other thing. The second step involved her addressing the messy middle, which would involve choosing platforms, data flow mapping, and organizations of all with project-management models.

Choosing the Right Tools

The engineering team has chosen the AWS S3 as a data lake. S3 is cheap, scalable and already compatible with the cloud services that the firm utilizes. JSON logs, IoT sensor feeds, etc. can all be stored in a bucket- no upfront schema required. Snowflake was the warehouse being looked at by finance and operations on the other hand. Snowflake is a highly scalable and cloud-native system with a legendary reputation of having efficient structured queries and dashboards.

The role of Emma was to be helpful in equalizing the dual-tool approach.

- AWS S3 (Lake)
  Advantages: Extremely cheap, flexible schema on read, best when applied to machine-learning processes.
  Weaknesses: There is no inbuilt governance (unless there are explicit rules) it will become a data swamp.
- Snowflake (Warehouse)

Strengths: Blistering queries, robust structured analytics, compliance ready.
Weaknesses: Cost of storage is high, requires defined schema at the start not good with unstructured data.

Instead of presenting these as opposing instruments, Emma has placed them in opposing positions. The raw stream of telemetry would be captured by S3 and the polished source of truth of ERP and reporting would be achieved via Snowflake.

Understanding ETL vs. ELT

Emma must have known ETL (Extract, Transform, Load) and ELT (Extract, Load, Transform) to make the dual system work. These acronyms came up casually to her engineering colleagues, but she was aware that project schedules were based on the difference.

- ETL (Warehouse-focused)
  The information is extracted out of source systems, cleansed, business-rule transformed and loaded into the warehouse. By the time it gets to Snowflake it is already structured, validated and dashboards are ready.
  Project effect: It involves initial planning, more lengthy pipelines and a close follow up with the stakeholders to establish transformation guidelines.
- ELT (Lake-focused)
  The information is mined and is directly loaded into the lake raw. The transformations occur subsequently, as they are requested or sent through data processing of the data by the analysts.
  Project impact: Pursues quicker, but flexibility is subject to the risk of the messy data in case of poor governance.

Regarding the project terminology, Emma described the difference:

ETL is the preparation and plating of the food prior to it being taken to the table. ELT can be compared to having all the groceries on the counter and later making decisions as to how to cook them.

Integrating Into Project Scope

Emma realized that storage decisions needed to be displaced out of the sphere of IT into the project plan. A Data Architecture Milestone was the new thing she has added to the logistics roadmap. The milestone included:

1. Repository Decisions: Go with S3 and Snowflake with buy-in among the stakeholders.
2. Pipeline Design: Determining which data streams are sent to the lake, which are sent to the warehouse and which require both.
3. Governance Standards: Creating naming standards, access controls and refresh cycles.
4. Testing and Validation: ETL jobs were executed in order to check data quality and then business users could depend on reports.

Standardizing this milestone pushed the structuring of data out of IT considerations and made it a project requirement.

Practical Applications in Project Workflows

Emma began to envision the impact the tools were going to have on day-to-day project management.

Sensors data on trucks Every day, the sensor data on trucks got ingested to S3. The raw feeds were pulled by the data scientists to predict maintenance and model the fuel efficiency. Project managers monitored the developments of these models in the innovation workstream.

- ERP Integration: Finance had nightly ETLs that inserted procurement and cost information into Snowflake and transformed the data into standardized tables. Emma established weekly reviews with Snowflake dashboards with stakeholders to provide executives with visibility.
- Hybrid Insights: Emma consulted with engineers when one of the executives questioned whether it was possible to make predictions about maintenance and correlate this data with cost predictions. They took out S3 sensor data features, transformed them and loaded them into Snowflake as well as ERP costs. The resultant picture showed that driving behavior had an impact on budget overruns.

These workflows proved that the two systems are not independent systems but collaborators in the story telling sense: the lake reveals possible insights, and the warehouse provides trusted reports.

Risk Management: Avoiding Data Swamps and Bottlenecks

Emma was also forced to prepare risks.

- Data Lake Risk: Lack of Governance: The lack of governance would allow the S3 bucket to become a data swamp - a disorganized pile of untagged files. Emma fixed this by establishing metadata rules: any file that entered the lake needed to have a set of tags, like source, timestamp and data owner.

- Warehouse Risk: There is a risk that snowflake pipelines could be bottlenecked in the event that transformation rules were not well understood. Emma averts this by including business stakeholders in the process of setting KPIs and reading sample reports to ensure scaling is done.

These protections resembled the classic project risk management: find your vulnerabilities early, lay ownership on them and construct contingency plans.

Communication With Non-Technical Stakeholders

Emma was frequently required to decode technical words into a basic project language. She developed an explainer in one page to the leadership team:

- S3 (Lake): imagine that it is our large storage box. It has everything here first--utopian, disorderly, and entire.
- Snowflake (Warehouse): "Grant it a name of our polished report library. Only structured data is permitted, which has been cleansed.
- ETL/ELT: Is it clean first, store it, or store first, clean it?

This made the language simple hence creating consistency in business, finance and engineering.

Lessons for Project Managers

The experience that Emma had provided some lessons to the managers who face such challenges:

1. Storage is tactical: The location of the data determines whether analytics are successful.
2. Hybrid tends to prevail: The majority of organizations enjoy the benefits of lakes and warehouses, it is not an either/or decision.
3. Make it concrete: Data architecture should not be backstage IT work, but a deliverable.
4. Governance ensures the absence of chaos: Swamps and bottlenecks are guarded by clear ownership and metadata rules.
5. Get bi-lingual: Managers are required to walk between the fine technical and executive lines.

Story Interlude: A Mini-Crisis

A problem occurred in the middle of implementation. A single team dropped thousands of CSV logs in the S3 lake and never labelled them correctly. The files had a mixture of date formats and missing identifiers and one more analyst attempted to query the files but found it all chaos.

Emma summoned an emergency meeting. She framed it as a governance gap instead of trying to blame the team. It is not that this is a case of one team committing errors, said she. It is the fact that we do not have clear rules. We need a data charter."

She has formulated a light-weight policy governing policy: a naming convention, a source system ID, and a validation check must be used with each upload. The policy was implemented and the lake got back into order. This crisis supported her as a protector of data operations, rather than a facilitator.

Looking Ahead to Metrics and Value

At the conclusion of the phase, Emma had implemented a working dual system: AWS S3 to explore, Snowflake to report, pipelines operating within ETL and ELT processes, and governance within the project plan.

But the story wasn't finished. The second difficulty was success measurement. That was how they would know whether the storage strategy was working or not? What KPIs would help demonstrate that the hybrid architecture was adding value?

Insights, Metrics, and Strategic Value

Emma was relieved to have achieved a project milestone by the time the AWS S3 and Snowflake were up and running by her team. However, soon she learned that the selection of tools was not everything. The actual task was to demonstrate that the hybrid system was able to provide business value. That is, would they be able to know whether their investment in a lake-and-warehouse architecture led to better results or not? The last stage was all about insights, measures and strategic alignment - the connection between storage and decision making.

Defining Success: The Role of Data Quality KPIs

Emma began by defining success using definite terms. She collaborated with engineering and finance to define data-quality KPIs that would make sure that the data was reliable. In the governance group the five dimensions were resolved:

1. **Completeness** Did they include all the necessary fields? Lack of truck IDs or blank cost centers may derail the analysis.
2. Consistency Were the values consistent across systems? (e.g., USA vs. United States).
3. Accuracy Did values represent reality? IoT temperature checks were compared to physical audits by spot checks.
4. **Timeliness Criterion- What was the freshness of the data? The updates of warehouses were required not to be older than 24 hours.
5. **Uniqueness** – Have there been duplicates deleted? There might be duplicate shipments that would include revenue figures.

These KPIs to Emma were not technical checks, but project-management checkpoints. As she had been monitoring milestones and budgets, she now monitored whether the information was fit to purpose.

Using Metrics to Drive Decisions

Having KPIs in place, Emma incorporated the data quality in project dashboards. For example:

- **IoT Monitoring** -When over 5 percent of sensor records were not complete, the system triggered corrective action to the operations team.

- **ERP Reports** - In case warehouse updates were delayed more than 48 hours, the finance department was alerted in time, prior to leadership meetings.

These performance measures established responsibility. Teams were no longer able to take data as correct and keep showing that it was. To Emma, this reflected earned-value management: the data governance was reflected in the scope, schedule and risk management.

The Strategic Value of Hybrid Architecture

The hybrid solution Emma came up with started to have real advantages:

1. **More Accelerated Insights** - Analysts can work with raw IoT data in S3 without weeks to design a schema streamlining innovation like predictive-maintenance testing.
2. **No Fake News** - Snowflake dashboards were believed by executives to be accurate and always reflect audited numbers of ERP. As well, decisions could be made without the customary caveats, which could be that the data could be off.
3. **Cross-Functional Views - The firm used to draw engineering benefits into the financial context by the extraction of features of the lake into the warehouse, such as fuel-efficiency trends based on cost overruns, which connects the result of engineering efforts to its financial consequences.

The architecture was discovered (lakes) as well as executed (warehouses) and allowed agility without any loss of control.

Avoiding Common Pitfalls

Emma also knew what not to do. Some pitfalls of the implementation were revealed:

- **The Data Swamp Threat** – S3 gurgled with files with poorly-labeled logs. Nothing could be found without a rigid tagging. Metadata standards held this under check.
- **Over-architecturing the Warehouse** - Other teams had raw IoT logs pushed into Snowflake to be complete. They were reminded by Emma that warehouses are intended to hold curated and structured data; all of that will slow queries and consume storage space.
- **Mismatched Expectations- Executives had originally desired real-time dashboards everywhere. Emma explained that nightly refreshing of some of the reports would have realistic expectations around timeliness versus cost.

These lessons have strengthened the fact that project managers need to be guardrails, rather than facilitators. Guardrails made the architecture remain sustainable.

Governance as a Strategic Lever

Emma learned that it wasn't a bureaucracy, but leverage that ruled the world. She incorporated metadata, validation, and access rights rules, thus establishing trust in the system. Her policy of ruling was:

- Each dataset was owned by a steward.
- Data that was ingested had timestamps and source IDs.
- Warehouse dashboards were found to pass monthly accuracy checks.

This administration transformed abstract data flows to dependable business assets. Stakeholders no longer argued about numbers but argued about actions, which became a cultural change and the most valuable result.

Measuring Project Impact

To convince the executive board of the value of the architecture Emma outlined three outcome metrics:

1. **Speed of decision making: It became possible to make cross functional reports in two days as compared to two weeks.
2. **Cost Efficiency** - Storage cost remained constant: raw logs remained cheap in S3, and high value structured data was stored in Snowflake.
3. **Adoption Rates**- Business teams now used dashboards on a weekly basis minimizing ad-hoc spreadsheets.

These measures reformulated the hybrid architecture as a business enabler, rather than as an IT project.

Story Interlude: The Quarterly Review

At the first quarterly review of the system since its launch, one of the main questions that the CEO posed was, What is behind our sudden spike in fuel costs this quarter?

In the past, this question would have led to an onslaught of emails to operations, hastily compiled spreadsheets, and discussion of which numbers could be relied upon. This time Emma opened a Snowflake dashboard which used the information of S3 lake.

The report found a clear trend; of the trucks that failed to pass the maintenance check-up, the level of fuel efficiency was significantly lower. The trend was revealed in raw IoT data, and the warehouse converted it into an estimate financial value.

The CEO reclined and smiled. Once I can believe the figures. But now only to determine what to do with them.

That was the point when Emma was convinced that the architecture was a success.

Key Insights for Project Managers

The story of Emma was condensed in a code of virtues:

1. Data Quality = Project Quality: The quality of analytics results is dependent on the quality of data. Consider data quality KPIs as normal project KPIs.
2. Balance Flexibility and Reliability: Discover with lakes and report with warehouses. The inefficiency comes about when one forcefully fits the other.
3. Governance is Cultural, not Just Technical: Ownership, metadata and validation create organizational trust.
4. Storage is Scope: Project managers need to incorporate data architecture in charters, milestones as well as risk registers.
5. Converse Results, Not Plumbing: Executives are concerned with how much faster and cheaper decisions are made and how much these decisions can be improved, rather than the plumbing involved ETL pipelines.

Closing the Chapter

The story of Emma being a confused coordinator to a self-assured data-driven leader showed that data lakes and warehouses are not luxuries in terms of technology but are necessities of a strategic nature. To the project managers, it is not about becoming an engineer but rather adding an element of data structure to project planning.

Data lakes leave the doors open to discovery in the future. The existing decision-making is being made on the solid system of data warehouses. They work collectively to help make disorganized and unstructured information into actionable intelligence.

In the case of the company of Emma, the hybrid architecture was no longer merely a tactic of storing the data, but also a competitive edge. And to Emma herself it was her passage to the next stage of co-ordinator to the next stage of strategist, one who was able to bridge the worlds of raw possibility and organised reality.

This tradeoff between lake and warehouse between flexibility and governance will determine more and more which projects fail and which succeed as projects become more data-intensive.

CHAPTER 4:

DATA LITERACY FOR NON-TECHNICAL PROFESSIONALS

…■…■…

Raj's Awakening to Data Literacy

Raj had established himself as a trusted project manager in maintaining people on track and projects on schedule. He was not the kind to be lost on the technical details, but instead he was interested in deadlines, budgets and intra-departmental communication. However, as his organization became more digital, he was finding that the language of project success was evolving. Gantt charts were no longer the order of the day during meetings but the order of the day then was dashboards and KPIs as well as performance analytics. He tended to smile broadly when one of the colleagues described a difference in cost per sprint or indicated a heat map which allegedly showed the risks of customer dissatisfaction. Raj was able to follow the discussion to the superficial level, but he did not have the courage to question assumptions and ask probing questions.

Privately, he experienced disconnect between the skills that he was able to master, and those that the new era of data-driven management required.

One such Monday morning he walked into a project steering committee meeting which was the turning point. The CIO had loaded a live Power BI dashboard of supplier performance and project throughput. Late deliveries were marked using colored bars, resources allocation was illustrated using pie charts and an upward trend line identified the increase in defect rates. Raj stuttered when a senior executive enquired about whether these delays were due to the inefficiency of the vendors or they were caused by internal scheduling bottlenecks. He was not able to differentiate what aspect of the visualization narrated that story. A very fast analyst jumped in to give a reply but Raj was made to feel down. He went out of the room determined to reform. He desired to read these dashboards himself, interpret the KPIs and to chair discussions confidently.

The initial understanding he had was that the non-technical-level data literacy was not about being able to master the code or sophisticated statistics. It was related to fluency representation the capacity to read, comprehend and convey the information that is integrated in graphs, measurements, and tables. Similar to the way that language literacy allows individuals to read books and make arguments, data literacy empowers professionals to read visualizations and frame evidence-based decisions. In its absence a project manager can easily turn into one who is reliant on others to interpret the data, lose credibility in leadership circles and miss risks that the numbers can silently tell her about. It gives it independence, power, and clarity to the project manager.

Raj began with the basics. He has revised key performance indicators, but this time as actual measurements rather than some abstract acronym. He had been covering on time delivery, variation of budget and resource use over the years but had seldom bothered to investigate how it was done. He now took time to learn. On-time delivery was a ratio: the number of tasks done on time or earlier in the schedule divided by the total number of tasks. Budget variance was a comparison of actual expenditure and planned expenditure commonly as a percentage. The use of resources was calculated in number of hours worked and number of hours available. Knowledge of these formulae brought him confidence. He no longer took a red or green light to be a judgment; he knew how that worked. This enabled him to question when measurement was deceptive and clarify their meaning in simple terms to his stakeholders.

Growing inquisitiveness made Raj resort to dashboards. Power BI was now a key tool in his company and some of the departments favored Google Data Studio due to its integration with the existing suite. Initially the dashboards appeared intimidating there was a mass of charts, filters and visuals that competed to capture attention. But Raj trained himself to think of all his visualizations as stories. A line chart that followed the change in cycle time on a weekly basis was not a curve, it was a testimony to the efficiency of the team in its handling of tasks. The bar chart of the vendor lead times was not only the groups of the rectangles; this was the story of the suppliers who were always on time and those who were creating bottlenecks. A heat map of the module-by module defects revealed a story of where the risks were concentrated. He did this by posing the question of what each visualization told him about his project, thus creating a habit of reducing the visuals to the stories that could be acted upon by the executives and teams.

Actual practice hastened his development. Raj started extracting dashboards of the earlier projects and reading them out as case studies. Viewing a two-year-old budget variance chart, he questioned himself as to why the costs had shot up in Q3. By comparing with meeting notes he got to know that scope creep had led to increase in resource hours. A velocity chart of an agile project indicated an unexpected downturn in the middle of a sprint, which he attributed to an unexpected non-availability of senior developers. These practices conditioned him not to view data as numbers but as the tracks of the real events. The more he practiced the more fluent he became.

With time, his self-confidence changed. During the team meetings, rather than waiting until analysts can speak, Raj started giving his interpretation. He would indicate a KPI and give an explanation of what that indication would mean regarding workflow, or a dashboard trend that indicated a risk. His co-workers realized the transformation. His skill to negotiate the complex world of technical images with a strategic language was valued by executives. His team members liked his clarity. In the case of Raj, fear of data had shifted to curiosity which had evolved to fluency.

Building Confidence Through Practice and Tools

Raj became more data-literate on his side, and realized that his colleagues shared an equivalent level of discomfort with him. Most of the non-technical team members were unable to read dashboards. Explanations of visualizations were frequently too technical or too abstract or too rushed when they were presented by analysts. Raj also understood that data literacy could not be an individual endeavor, but it must be a team competency within the project setting. Without the ability of teams and stakeholders to read and interpret data, then their cooperation would never be complete.

In response to this, Raj suggested an organized program: consider data literacy a formal project deliverable. Since they are going to train on new software systems, he claimed that they should also train on how to make sense of the data generated by these systems. His concept appealed due to the fact that it fulfilled an increasing organizational requirement. There are enormous volumes of metrics created by projects, yet numerous decision makers are unable to navigate them. Raj made literacy training not optional but a necessary part of the project by making it part of the scope of work.

His designs of workshops were based on real life scenarios. During a single session he displayed a PowerBI dashboard and requested respondents to explain what they were looking at. Instead of bombarding them with definitions he made them ask questions: Why does this line trend up? What could be the reason of this outlier? Which departments will get impacted most with this heat map? To the extent that these questions created confidence and demonstrated that literacy is not memorizing formulas, but engaging critically with the data.

Another exercise that was introduced by Raj was the reconstruction of project stories on the previous dashboards in small groups. They were given anonymized measures in terms of cycle time, defects, sprint velocity and tasked with a narration of what could have occurred. Teams were inclined to find plausible explanations which were consistent with real events. These exercises strengthened the fact that numbers are not abstract, they are realistic choices, actions and limitations. Stating the importance of literacy in connection with the lived experiences, the participants assimilated the value of literacy.

Especially in these exercises, powerBI came in handy. Its interactivity enabled the participants to drill down, filter by department or switch to a different type of visual. Raj went through them switching filters and how the same data can have different stories depending on the lens. The simplicity of Google Data Studio, which enhanced the message that simply anyone, not only analysts could create simple dashboards. It is possible to break the myth of data being the property of specialists with the help of such tools as visualization which Raj demonstrated to be available to everyone.

One of the strongest changes took place when the participants understood that literacy is questionable, not an Aha! moment. Raj told me that there is nothing wrong with not understanding the reason why a trend emerges at first. The art is to observe the trend, propose potential causes and to know whom to consult to gain a more in-depth understanding. This strategy made a psychological safety. There was no more fear of being wrong among team members, they felt strong enough to participate. In the course of time, such cultural change diminished the silent passivity that prevailed during meetings at the time dashboards used to be shown. Discussions were interactive with varying voices where attributing meanings was involved.

Raj also urged his fellow team to train. To integrate data drills into weekly meetings, he chose a chart and asked all of them to provide a brief interpretation. This was done within a period of less than five minutes and retrained fluency. First the responses were provisional and disjointed. As time passed by, they sharpened and the participants were able to relate metrics and tie them to project results. It is a very basic practice that changed the relationship of the team with data, incorporating the idea of literacy into the workflow.

The result became evident when Raj was present at another executive review a few months later. When the COO inquired regarding increasing vendor delays, Raj was able to produce a dashboard, tried out some filtering, and told him that two suppliers were always late because of disruption of transport in their region. He put the numbers in terms of realities of operations and suggested mitigation measures. Executives reacted favorably stating that Raj was now a mature leader who had the ability to bridge analysis and decision. What was more important, his team was already at a stage where it could make a significant contribution to such discussions. The literacy initiative had brought the whole project environment to a higher level.

Embedding Data Literacy as a Project Imperative

The long-term advantages of data literacy to the organization of which Raj works were realized. The use of data was democratized and projects no longer relied on a small number of analysts. As executives realized, it was now quicker and more informed to make decisions since managers such as Raj could access dashboards through direct reading. There was less time wastage in teams having to reconcile conflicting numbers as teams knew the structure and meaning of KPI. Instead of debating over spreadsheets they argued on what to do because they used common evidence. This cultural maturity made the organization nimble in a world with more data driven projects.

The change that Raj underwent was radical. He was no longer sidelined in the technical discussions but he led as a confident person. The shift was not based on learning how to program or even learning machine learning, but on becoming data literate, or knowing how to read, interpret, and communicate data. As he demonstrates, non-technicals should not be afraid of analytics. They can invest in literacy, which would help increase their leadership and increase their influence.

Raj also increased his project-management capabilities with the help of data literacy. In risk management he estimated possible delays, and derived probabilities based on past statistics. He converted dashboards to stories that were comprehended by the executives in stakeholder communication. He identified signs of variances in the budgeting rather than waiting until the end of the month to find out. Literacy did not exist as an independent skill; it increased the scale of his job in all respects.

In order to support the progress, Raj promoted constant learning. He encouraged co-workers to apply data instruments in the same way they applied project-management applications-application that develops and requires practice. He encouraged mentorship: non-technical employees were mentored by analysts, who provided an operational backdrop. This mutuality resulted in the common ownership of insights. Governance was also imposed by Raj, and dashboards were required to reveal data sources and refresh rates and constraints. He forced transparency, hence preventing confusion and creating trust in the figures.

The most impressive result was the dynamics in the team. Meetings that used to be filled with technical voices were transformed into participative and sharing grounds where everyone provided an interpretation. A business analyst might indicate trends in customer comments, a project manager connected the trends with the delivery times, and a programmer connected them with the system functionality. This cross-pollination resulted in more discussions and decisions. Literacy broke down silos and brought the various roles together through the same evidence.

Finally, the story of Raj demonstrates that data literacy is a crucial part of the contemporary project management. It is essential like communication, scheduling or budgeting. There will be an ever-increasing volume of data and without literacy professionals, they are likely to be submerged in the vast numbers of data that they will not be able to understand. Literacy brings with it clarity, foresight and authority. Power BI and Google Data Studio can help, but it is the attitude of mindfulness, practice, and readiness to interact that can actually make change.

Raj came to realise that dashboard numbers do not frighten, they are the story of performance, risk, and opportunity. Through reading such stories, he has empowered his organization and team and boosted his leadership. His trip offers a rallying cry to all non-technical professionals: cease being active data consumers. Be engaged as interpreters, questioners, and narrators. Data literacy is turning projects into not a guesswork effort but one based on evidence and making managers confident leaders.

Those who mediate between people, process and data are the future of project management. Raj demonstrated that that role can be played by anybody who does not have a technical background. His narrative proves the fact that literacy is not the matter of complicacy- it is the matter of clarity. Clarity leads to the creation of trust, strategy, and sustainable success in a data-driven world when adopted by project managers and teams.

CHAPTER 5:

PREDICTIVE ANALYTICS FOR STRATEGIC DECISION-MAKING

…■…■…

Lisa's Journey into Predictive Analytics

Lisa Chen had a reputation as a no-nonsense project manager in the middle of a busy logistics company that was based in Chicago. She had eight years of experience leading complex supply-chain transformations using Gantt charts, stakeholder alignments and contingency buffers. By experience and intuition, she was always a step ahead of the pitfalls she might have fallen into. However, when, in the fall of 2024, her team started working on an enormous project of warehouse automation, covering numerous premises, Lisa encountered a challenge that could not be addressed entirely using her conventional toolkit. The project also required the addition of robots, overhauling inventory programs, and retraining of the personnel staff- all under the variable delivery schedule of the vendors, and the erratic shortage of labor due to the continuous economic changes.

The first few weeks were encouraging. Targets were achieved, and expenses remained low and the team was buzzing. Then subtle cracks appeared. One of the major suppliers was late by one week in supplying the components, citing disruptions to the supply chains. Two experienced engineers got sick at one of the critical integration points, which left the rest of the staff stretched. The weekly status reports of Lisa were alright but her hunch told her she was not. Time was lost in driblets, two days here and three there and the allocation of resources was like a game of dice. We are moving too slowly and later she was heard saying that to her deputy on a late night review. When we notice the delay, it is costing us thousands.

Lisa was exposed to predictive analytics in a practical sense after a company-wide webinar on the latest trends in technology. The speaker was a consultant at a competitor company who described an example of predictive models predicting project slips 85 percent of the time to enable teams to redistribute resources before failure occurred. Curiosity led Lisa to the research that evening where she read articles and tutorials. She understood that predictive analytics was not magic of data gurus; it was a systematic approach to make use of the past data to forecast the future. To project managers, it offered the ability to move away to reactive firefighting to proactive strategy.

The following day Lisa volunteered a pilot to her team. They would construct a simple model to predict the possible delays in the basis of historical project data. Cynicism spread over the room--most of them were not technical, and models sounded terrifying. I am not requesting us to be programmers, Lisa promised them. This is concerning making our decisions evidence based. They began with small projects, one taking the data on the past five analogous projects: the variables such as the number of resource hours recorded, the rating of difficulty of the task (the score was 1-10 depending on the number of dependencies and technical difficulties), the scores of the vendor reliability, and the number of delayed days.

Patterns came out as they entered this data into a simple tool. Delays of 57 days were usually associated with high task complexity and extended resource hours. With the model being trained, it was able to forecast a 60 per cent possibility of a 4 day slip in the subsequent phase in case staffing was not changed. With this, Lisa diverted two junior analysts who were working on a low-priority task to assist the integration team. She further bargained buffer stock with the supplier using the forecast of the model as leverage.

The results were eye-opening. The phase accomplished on schedule, 8 per cent below budget and team morale went so high because they could see information influence their wins. Lisa didn't stop there. She repeated the model, introducing time-series terms in order to consider seasonal labor variations. In a short time, predictive analytics became a regular part of their weekly huddles, and it enabled better allocation of resources by identifying those who were overworked before burnout. The case of Lisa depicts a very deep realization that in the world of uncertainty, predictive tools simply do not substitute human judgment, instead, they enhance it and transform project management into a futuristic discipline.

The project also minimized the delays occurring by 22 percent of the historical averages, and the team headed by Lisa saved the company more than $150 k in overtime and fines. Her epiphany? Predictive analytics closes the divide between what has been learned in the past and what will be done in the future, and thus strategic decision-making is not only informed, but also prescient. It is an instrument that any project manager can use to maneuver through complexity just like Sarah, Tom, Emma and Raj in the earlier chapters of this book, all of them using data to their own advantage towards success..

Understanding Predictive Analytics

Predictive analytics is one of the pillars of the development of data-based project management that should provide a logical method of predicting the future consequences based on the behavioral tendencies of the past. It is fundamentally based on applying statistical algorithms and machine learning to predict the probability of occurrence of future events, which will provide managers with an opportunity to make an informed decision making it possible not to rely only on experience or guessing. Applying this to projects, this can be viewed as the prediction of delays, budget overruns or resource bottlenecks that can be prevented before they become problems.

In order to understand its basics, it is worth first looking at the major approaches which include regression analysis, time-series forecasting, and machine learning models. Regression, which is arguably the easiest point of entry into the field that non-technical professionals can make, is a study of how variables interact. Linear regression, as an example, presupposes a linear relationship -e.g. between the amount of resource hours spent and the days of delay of a project. It is easy to understand: the more hours generally decrease delays, the higher the order of connection the model measures, which can be used to predict, such as, "Three days of delays can be reduced by adding 50 more hours of work to the project model). It is further elaborated by multiple regression that considers various factors, including the level of task difficulty or the level of experience within the team, giving a more detailed picture.

The steps of time-series analysis work when the data is time-dimensional and is often utilized in the projects that have a staged character. This approach examines time series such as weekly progress reports or monthly budgets to identify trends, seasonality or cycles. Such tools as ARIMA (AutoRegressive Integrated Moving Average) may be used to predict the further points in accordance with the old tendencies, i.e. to predict the more significant delay risks in the period of the holidays when the vendor responsiveness drops. It is especially useful in long-term projects in which historical data is stored, and real-time changes can be made.

The machine learning models take this a notch higher by managing non-linear relationships that could have otherwise not been realized by traditional statistics. Learning algorithms (usually decision tree or random forest) are supervised with labeled data (e.g. past projects with delay outcomes labeled) to make a classification (or prediction) of a new scenario. A subdivision, neural networks, imitates the human brain patterns to be able to gain even greater understanding, but more data and computing power are needed. Unsupervised learning, such as clustering, provides groupings of similar phases of project to reveal hidden threats without prior determination of results.

The connection between these is their quality data dependency. Predictive analytics is not magic; it is mathematics on evidence. Regression was used in the case of Lisa to quantify the effect of the resource hours and the complexity of the tasks on the delays and a time-series element was used to explain project progression with each week. To project managers, the beauty of it is that it is practical: it turns unspecified fears (What if we fall behind?) into specifiable possibilities (There is 70% chance we will delay if we do not reallocate now).

Most importantly, predictive analytics requires consideration of ethics. Historical bias, such as whether previous projects have underscored some group of team members, may contribute to inequity in projections. Managers have to prove models in terms of different situations and make sure that the derivation of predictions is transparent. In addition, it is not always true; external influences such as economic recessions can shake even the most perfect models, which provokes the necessity of human control.

This chapter advances the more fundamental themes that were developed in assessing the greater volume of the book. As Sarah did in Chapter 1, integrating analytics in making decisions, and Tom did in Chapter 2, consolidating data that had been scattered, predictive tools here do the same, but in projecting forward. The storage support of these data lakes and warehouses offered by Emma and the literacy focus of Raj make non-technical users interpret model outputs. The book puts forward the intellectual assumption that project management is no longer dynamic but dynamic with predictive analytics being the driver of strategic foresight. It teaches readers to look at data as a core competency rather than a back office activity, which encourages them to think that anticipation is better than response.

The Process of Building Predictive Models

The predictive modeling is an iterative and planned process that resembles formal stages of project management itself: planning, implementation, monitoring, and improvement. It starts with the collection of data, and the keystone of all other things. This is a step that includes the collection of the historical data of various sources project logs, timesheets, vendor reports, performance measurements. The first thing is quality; any incomplete or noisy data will result in unreliable forecasts. In the pilot Lisa provided, her team developed a dataset based on previous projects, but added such variables as resource hours (amount of effort logged in total), familiarity with task (subjective but standardized score), and results (delays days). To reduce errors, to the extent possible, they cross-verified the entries against real reports, and a single source of truth is required as mentioned in the previous chapters.

Next, there is feature engineering, an imaginative but analytical stage during which raw data gets converted into valuable inputs to be used in the model. The variables that are used to make predictions are called features- consider them as building blocks. This may include establishing new ones such as considering a ratio of complexity-hours such as dividing task complexity by resource hours to reflect interactions. The most important steps to prevent skewing of results is normalization (scaling values to a common range) and dealing with missing data (imputing averages or dropping rows). Extreme cases, e.g., a delay caused by a rare event, need to be considered: consider them representative, or treat them as an outlier. The team at Lisa devised features that included classifying tasks as low, medium and high complexity and then matched them with delay data, and found that high complexity tasks increased risks of delays when there were low hours.

This is followed by model building, in which the algorithm selected is used to analyze the ready data. Begin with simple: with regression problems such as predicting delay days, linear regression is used to fit a straight line to reduce errors between the predicted and actual value. This is made available to novices in Python by using libraries such as scikit-learn.. Here's a sample implementation based on Lisa's approach:

import pandas as pd from sklearn.linear_model import LinearRegression from sklearn.model_selection import train_test_split from sklearn.metrics import mean_squared_error

Load data

data = pd.read_csv('project_data.csv')

Feature selection

X = data[['resource_hours', 'task_complexity']] y = data['project_delay_days']

Split into training and testing sets

X_train, X_test, y_train, y_test = train_test_split(X, y, test_size=0.2, random_state=42)

Build and train model

model = LinearRegression() model.fit(X_train, y_train)

Make predictions

predictions = model.predict(X_test)

Evaluate

mse = mean_squared_error(y_test, predictions) print(f'Mean Squared Error: {mse}')

The code reads a CSV file, picks features, separates data (80 percent to train and 20 percent to test in order to prevent overfitting), trains the model, predicts on unknown data, and measures accuracy in terms of mean squared error (smaller is better). In the case of time-series, such libraries as statsmodels can be used to provide ARIMA: import statsmodels.tsa.arima.model ARIMA(data[delays], order=111)).fit; forecast = model.forecast(steps=5).

Machine learning opens possibilities: random forests are used to deal with non-linearities through the generation of many decision trees and averaging the outcome. In scikit-learn: import sklearn.ensemble as randomforestregressor; rf_model = randomforestregressor(n_estimators=100).fit(X_train, y_train). Hyperparameter optimization The performance is optimized through hyperparameter tuning, such as changing the number of trees, typically including grid search.

The gatekeeper is evaluation, where the model may not be memorizing data as generalizing. The measures are metric: in regression, the root mean squared error is used to measure the deviation of the prediction; in classification (e.g., delay vs. no delay) accuracy or F1-score (balance between precision and recall). Cross-validation -it is the repetition and splitting and testing of data to protect against flukes. Here, the team of Lisa refined and refined until reliable forecasting was attained.

It is aided by tools: the ecosystem of Python (equipped with pandas to manipulate data, scikit-learn to model it) is free and efficient. Jupyter Notebook is both an interactive writing workspace and a canvas to experiment, and one can edit code, graphics, and notes all in a single file, which is the best way to share with a team. To be visualized, Power BI is fully compatible: it accepts predictions as a data source, and one can draw line charts, illustrating forecasted and actual delays, or heat maps, indicating the areas of risk. Lisa did her prototyping in Jupyter, and plotted the results in Power BI dashboards to be reviewed by the stakeholders.

This process has an intellectual implication in the thesis stated in the book that data analytics democratizes expertise. Lisa, a non-technical manager, can be the overall in charge of model-building and concentrates on business logic, defining features and interpreting outputs, but is collaborating with the technical peers. It resembles the literacy drive by Raj: being able to know how to do something makes one feel confident, so that one does not get caught in the black-box. More importantly, the book assesses conventional methods of project to be inadequate in volatile environment; predictive modeling provides a sense of rigor, quantifying uncertainties that intuition cannot provide. Nevertheless, it comes with a caution that models have not been prophetic but probabilistic and hence they require constant reaffirmation with real-life changes..

Integrating Predictive Analytics into Project Management

The incorporation of predictive analytics in the project management process makes it more of a strategy, especially in risk management. In the traditional risk plans, the threats are identified qualitatively, high, medium, low, through the experience of the experts. They are measured using predictive models, which assign probabilities and impacts, which allows prioritized responses. In the project proposed by Lisa, the model was included in the risk register: estimated delays led to automatic notifications, which caused mitigation measures such as the switch of resources. Such proactive behavior is also within the standards of PMI, and improves the risk response planning stage.

In reality, begin by mapping models to project lifecycle stages. During initiation, use history information to forecast the general duration/cost variation. In the planning, predict the required resources through time-series of workload trends. It takes advantage of real-time predictions: feed real-time data into the models to make changes on a weekly basis to modify the schedules. Monitoring and controlling entail dashboards of prediction accuracy, model refinement during the project. Reviews of actual and anticipated outcomes are made on closure to feed information into the data pool to enhance additional accuracy in the future.

Difficulties emerge: transfer learning (applying the models to other domains) is needed due to a lack of data in new projects. Interpretability is important - opaque complex ML models such as neural networks are not easy to interpret; simpler models such as regression provide coefficients of variable effects (e.g. Each complexity point adds 1.2 delay days). Create a sense of buy-in by the team: make the models seem like a tool and not an oracle.

This is the intellectual point of convergence of the book: the revelation of Sarah about the power of analytics, the unity of data, and the literacy and to predictive foresight. It considers project management as a cross-disciplinary science, involving a combination of human intuition and computational accuracy. The success of Lisa is an example of this synergy, which decreases doubts and increases effects. Finally, predictive analytics enables managers to be evidence-led in their efforts to make sure that projects are not just being successful in a volatile world but are excellent.

CHAPTER 6

REAL-TIME ANALYTICS FOR AGILE PROJECTS

Mark's Leap into Real-Time Clarity

Mark Rivera, an experienced Scrum Master at a rapidly expanding fintech start-up in New York had spent twelve years perfecting the Scrum project management. His days used to be made up of facilitating daily stand-ups, solving team blockers and making sure that sprints provided a value within the tight two week cycles. Mark was reputed to be good in the turbulent environment of Agile where cross-functional teams of developers, designers and product owners had to be kept on track. However, during the spring of 2025, when his company was expanding its mobile banking application to cover millions of users in North America, Mark faced one of the problems that pushed his usual practices to their limits: the information that informed his decisions was always one step behind.

The project under consideration was a massive one the implementation of the biometric authentication and real-time fraud detection into the app, with a deadline preconditioned by the regulatory pressure and the market competition. The team tracked tasks through Jira, managed the code through GitHub and communicated via Slack, and their initial sprint plans were strong. Burndown charts were predicted to show gradual improvement, story points were carefully estimated and stakeholders were positive. However, when the first sprint took place, cracks developed. Frontend work was slowed because a backend developer had reached a dead end on an API integration bug. On the basis of user testing feedback, priorities changed within the mid-sprint, although by the time Mark got around to compiling updates based on emails and stand-up notes, critical hours would have been lost. The frozen Excel reports on which he had been depending were like rubbish--true yesterday, useless to-day.

Mark was frustrated and during a late-night review he told his product owner that they were always playing catch-up. Before we even see a problem, it is already derailing us because we see it. The breakthrough point came as a surprise after an innovation summit of the company, which invited a guest speaker who presented real-time analytics dashboards that were transforming Agile workflows. The case study pointed to a retail technology company that shortened sprint time by 28 percent in live data feeds to re-prioritize on a fly basis. Interested, Mark passed the evening into online forums and tutorials and found out how applications such as

Tableau and Power BI can pull in data in real time via applications like Jira or IoT sensors and give a real-time pulse on project health.

Mark offered the following day a pilot to his crew. Suppose we could have a dashboard that would tell us every hour where we are, how much we have burndown, how fast we are going, how evenly our teams are working, etc. Cynicism spread across the room; a large number of staff members, particularly the non-technical staff, were concerned about creating another load in an already overloaded workflow. A designer complained, "We are not data scientists. Mark had to assure them: That is no code. It is having a clear view of our work and working quicker. Their initial project was tiny and took Jira (task statuses and story points), GitHub (frequency of commits) and Slack(communication patterns) data through a single dashboard using Power BI. The installation required one weekend, and I used the assistance of a junior analyst who set up API webhooks to get real-time updates.

The impact was immediate. A chart of corrupted burndown during the following stand-up showed that there was a bottleneck--tasks in the "in review column were clogging and marked in red. Going deep into the data, Mark realized that a QA engineer was overwhelmed with testing tickets. He reallocated one of the developers to help and the backlog was cleared in a few hours. A different dashboard indicated a decrease in speed, which was predicted by too many Slack threads; a brief team meeting decreased the workload on the meeting, and increased the time of concentration. At the end of the sprint, the team provided all the promised stories and a bonus UI enhancement and was highly appreciated by the stakeholders. The retrospective felt excited as the team members spoke of the clarity with one member of the development team stating, that it felt like they were driving with GPS rather than a paper map.

The experiment of Mark developed into a routine. KPIs such as cycle time (task start to finish) and defect density, which were typically planned in real time, were made central parts of the sprint planning. There were automated alerts that sent pings when the metrics reached a threshold, such as a 20% decline in commits, and an action was taken. The team also spent 15 hours per week less on manual reporting and after three months, the team had 25 percent higher sprint success rates. The story of Mark is a reflection of the larger reality: in the high-stakes, data-saturated world of the future, the application of real-time analytics turns Agile into a reactive approach and a proactive force. It is a continuation of the analytics adoption by Sarah in Chapter 1, data consolidation by Tom in Chapter 2, storage strategies by Emma in Chapter 3, the push of literacy by Raj in Chapter 4 and predictive foresight by Lisa in Chapter 5. Intellectually, this chapter assesses the developmental trend of the book project management is a dynamic, evidence-based field whose real-time tools enable managers to manage complexity with accuracy, so that agility is not a buzzword or a myth, but an objective fact..

The Power of Real-Time Analytics in Agile and SCRUM

Real-time analytics is an accessibility that will be a game-changer in Agile and SCRUM settings since it fits well in the original principles of the methodologies of adaptability, collaboration, and continuous improvement. Real-time analytics works in contrast to the traditional batch processing where the data is summarized and evaluated regularly (daily or weekly), and data is generated immediately and viewed to provide immediate insights. This immediacy in Agile, where the speed of iterating and keeping up with change is crucial, transforms abstract measures into practical directions. These advantages are enhanced by SCRUM and its segmented sprints, daily stand-ups, and retrospectives by incorporating live-data into each ceremony, making decisions quicker and more accurate.

Improved Visibility and Transparency The first short-term advantage is visibility. Agile teams are lightweight and need transparency, whereas fixed tools such as printed burndown charts or end-day reports are out of step with reality. Real-time analytics can continually show progress of such sources as issue trackers (Jira, Trello) or code repositories (GitHub, GitLab) with updates being shown in dashboards that are updated every one minute. A live burndown chart, e.g., is an example that illustrates the story points that have been done and those that have not yet been done, and there will be color-coded indicators to alert about any same-stalled tasks. In SCRUM, it implies that daily stand-ups are changed in the form of not telling what has been done yesterday but of live blockers. A PMI survey in 2025 had also revealed that teams with real-time dashboards had reduced blocker resolution time by 30 percent because a problem such as delayed code review is flagged immediately. Such transparency creates trust, as the stakeholders will witness the progress occurring, which reflects what Raj stressed, namely using data as a means of understanding.

The response to change more than sticking to a plan is the mantra of the Proactive Decision-Making Agile, which is dependent on timely information. Immediate KPIs, including cycle time, lead time, or defect rates, enable teams to prevent problems that arise. Take a SCRUM team that realizes that the number of bugs reported is increasing in the middle of the sprint through a live dashboard, they can de-emphasize new features and focus on testing to avoid quality crisis. In the example of Mark, real-time velocity checks showed that he was making philanthropic contributions to productivity, which were immediately adjusted in the schedule. Such a proactive response can be seen as the waste reduction as proposed by Lean, as reworking is minimized. Data in the industry in 2025 indicates that Agile real-time analytics teams are 20 percent more successful in sprinting because decisions are made based on evidence rather than gut feelings. This is based on the predictive models created by Lisa, which predicts risks and real-time analytics allows responding to the risk immediately.

Enhanced Teamwork SCRUM is based on cross-functional teams, yet the information silos may split the teamwork. Real-time analytics removes these barriers, giving an output of a shared, live project health view. Code commit trends are visible to developers, and the testing progress of the QA is visible to code developers; the product owner can see user feedback metrics provided by the beta tests. Tableau or power BI dashboards become the single source of truth, which could be accessed by everyone. This is essential in

2025 remote-heavy work environment remote teams are always in-step will not wait until experienced in an email update. An example is a product owner that changes the sprint priorities based on the live user data to make sure that the developers work on the features that will have the greatest impact. Such inclusiveness minimizes miscommunication, which saves such re-work up to 15 percent as reported by the current Agile Alliance. It resembles the data consolidation of Tom, so that every voice will be involved in a single story.

Dynamic Risk Management Risk management The Agile approach to risk management tends to be reactive- problems are raised during retrospectives or sprint reviews. This is changed to real-time analytics. Algorithms that detect anomalies, built into such tools as BigQuery, identify irregularities, such as an abrupt decrease in speed or a sharp increase in defects, and send alerts. This enables changes in the middle of the sprint, e.g. in SCRUM, giving lower priority to potentially risky stories to guard the committed backlog. Mark, through his team, monitored alerts in order to avoid delays by catching QA overload before it set in. This proactive method improves the confidence of the stakeholders as the 2025 data records an increase of 25 percent in the real-time delivered teams that are equipped with real-time. It is a complement to Lisa predictive analytics where forecasts prepare the stage, and reality data makes things happen.

Scalability and Compliance Scalable projects Scale Global projects that traverse millions of transactions, such as the app Mark was working on, require manual tracking which breaks down as the project grows larger. Instant pipelines analyze large volumes of data (APIs or IoT devices) in real time, meaning that the insights will keep up with the expansion. Live auditing is used in regulated industries such as fintech where data is used in real-time, and dashboards are used to ensure that the data is used according to the requirements of other regulations, such as GDPR or PCI-DSS. This scalability is related to the data lakes and warehouses of Emma, in which the effective storage of data streamlines data flow. Theoretically, the book assesses real-time analytics as the logical culmination of its data-driven thesis: since Sarah first hugged each other, to Mark live dashboards, it makes Agile a reactive ecosystem so that managers can coordinate results but not guesses..

Tools for Real-Time Analytics Success

Real-time analytics is essential in Agile projects and the tools to unlock it are imperative. Tableau, Power BI, and Google BigQuery are highlighted in the year 2025 due to its capability to process the live data, be integrated with the Agile workflow, and provide the actionable visualization. All of them have their advantages, depending on various project requirements, and the latest updates make them more suitable to the iterative nature of SCRUM.

Tableau: Visual Storytelling at Speed Tableau is known to develop user-friendly real-time visualizations that can appeal to Agile organizations. In 2025.2, it added Concierge, which supports natural language queries on live data e.g. Show sprint velocity trends this week. This gives the non-technical users power, which can be aligned with the literacy push by Raj. Hyper reduces latency to just a few seconds to retrieve information on APIs or databases such as Jira. Analytics pane is a feature of Tableau that makes it easy to add a trend line or prediction on the live burndown charts, which are best suited to SCRUM stand-ups. In the case of Mark, Tableau and Slack integration allowed the team to get real-time updates of issues, such as the declining velocity, in team channels. Tableau App on Google Workspace allows co-editing dashing, which is essential in remote Agile teams. Privacy: Private Closet gives the data the necessary security, which is crucial in fintech regulation. Although Tableau has prices that are more applicable to larger companies, the learning curve would need some initial training, though the visual presentation is popular among stakeholders presentations.

Power BI: Combined and AI-Powered The Power BI by Microsoft works well in environments where they are using Azure or Teams already, which is prevalent among startups such as that of Mark. The September 2025 update improved live edit on semantic models, which allows teams to adjust KPIs (e.g., cycle time) without rebuild of dashboards. The AI used by Copilot makes real-time summaries, such as Backend tasks are slow because of API errors, which save time during stand-ups. Automatic Page Refresh and Streaming allow user to see the real-time images that are updated every few seconds and use sources such as GitHub or IoT feeds. The DAX language that is used by Power BI has the ability to support the creation of custom KPIs including real-time defect density which can be customized to sprint objectives. Its Fabric integration brings together fragmented data sources, which is similar to what Tom did.

To Agile managers, forecasting sprint risks with predictive analytics in Power BI (an extension of Chapter 5) is cost-effective, as it is free with basic features and priced at a premium with advanced features, which are less expensive than promoting their growing firms. Integrating loops can enhance cooperation, as teams will be able to work with current insights.

Google BigQuery: Scalable Backend Power BigQuery is the choice when working with large continuous datasets, including Agile projects whose data is generated by IoT or API. Its 2025 updates announced at Google Next contain continuous queries to run SQLs in real-time, which is ideal in following sprint metrics such as commit frequency. BigQuery Omni can query both clouds without moving the data, which allows using hybrid configurations. AI-based anomaly detectors alert against anomalies such as spikes in defects, making it possible to make fast SCRUM changes. SAP Business Data Cloud Connect unites business data and upgraded BI tools have conversational interfaces e.g. What is our lead time today? BigQuery is a serverless model that is easily scalable, and the pay-as-you-go type is suitable to dynamic projects. In the case of Mark, the application of BigQuery might be used to stream IoT data of the app performance monitors, and feed dashboards aiding real-time user experience data. Its zero copy access makes compliance possible, and this is essential to regulated industries.

The right fit tableau gives importance to visual storytelling, power BI gives importancc to Microsoft-centric integration, and BigQuery is important in scaling the big data. These tools are used to fill the necessary difference between simple analytics (Chapter 1) and real-time mastery to help managers approach data as a dynamic resource. It will be selected basing on the size of the team, amount of data, and the current infrastructure; Mark startup relied on Power BI because the tool was cheap and integrated with Jira, and larger businesses may want more polish in Tableau or the capacity of BigQuery.

Real-Time Pipelines and Agile Insights are two constituents of building.

The technical basis of Agile analytics has to be the implementation of real-time data pipelines through which the data flows can be moving smoothly through the sources into the dashboards. This can be done by retrieving data in APIs (e.g. Jira REST API) or IoT devices (e.g. MQTT sensors in development environments), normalizing it and loading it into visualizational tools. In 2025, it would be simplified by apps such as Apache Kafka, AWS Kinesis, or Google Cloud Dataflow, and democratised using low-code tools such as Estuary or Striim.

Pipeline Setup Steps

1. **Source Identification**: Map data sources—Jira for task statuses, GitHub for commits, IoT for performance metrics. Secure API keys or MQTT endpoints.
2. **Extraction**: Use webhooks for APIs (e.g., Jira updates trigger instant pushes) or IoT protocols like Pub/Sub for sensor streams. FineDatalink, updated in 2025, simplifies IoT integration.

3. **Transformation**: Clean data in-stream using Spark or Dataflow—standardize formats (e.g., dates as YYYY-MM-DD) and tag with metadata (source, timestamp). This prevents swamps, as Emma cautioned.
4. **Loading**: Stream to BigQuery or a database, then visualize in Tableau/Power BI. Continuous queries in BigQuery process live data, while Power BI's Streaming mode refreshes visuals instantly.
5. **Governance**: Implement validation (e.g., check for missing task IDs) and access controls to ensure compliance. Metadata tagging, as in Chapter 3, maintains order.

Example in Action: An example in 2025 Redpanda demonstrates the following: a tech company is streaming IoT telemetry on app servers to BigQuery using Kafka, identifying bottlenecks in the performance in real-time. This was reflected in the team created by Mark where Jira webhook was connected to Power BI in which the updates on tasks are displayed in real-time in a burndown chart. A loss of velocity brought out an alert that led to a stand-up discussion, overcoming a blocker in a few hours.

PMI takeaway: RT KPI changes SCRUM ceremonies. Burndown rate monitors hourly progress, which allows prioritization of a story to be changed during mid-sprints, e.g., a defect-spiking story that is deprioritized. Cycle time points out inefficiencies, such as long reviews, which cause a shift in resources. Lead time keeps the owners of products informed on the speed of delivery, which goes well with the needs of the users. In the case of Domo 2025, there are automated warning messages that indicate anomalies (e.g., 10 percent drop in velocity), which provide a pivot in time. These KPIs reduced the time to report by 15 hours per week in the project paper by Mark, and increased the sprint throughput by 20%.

Connection to the Arc of the Book: This chapter brings the book to its conclusions: since the analytics epiphany of Sarah, to the real-time mastery of Mark, the chapter assesses project management as a discipline based on data. The real-time analytics is on the basis of the consolidation of Tom, the architecture of Emma, the literacy of Raj, and the predictions of Lisa that Agile managers should be viewed as the strategic orchestration. In 2025 when change is the order of the day, these tools will not only adapt the projects, but will flourish and bring value with accuracy and confidence.

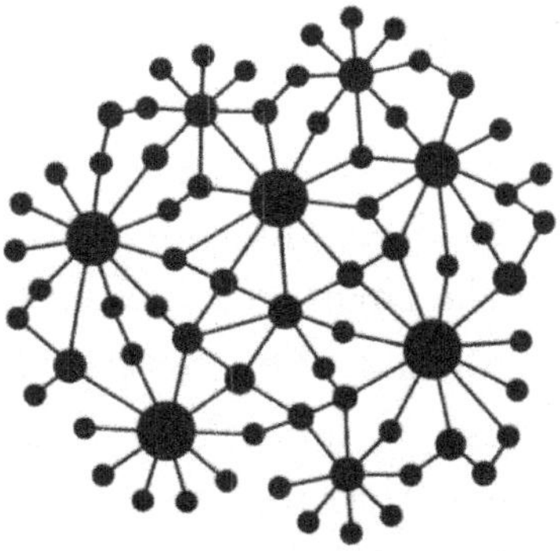

CHAPTER 7

ERP SYSTEMS AND ANALYTICS INTEGRATION

Having been hired as the project manager in the multinational engineering company, Ms. Priya Patel quickly realized that personnel management was not the major problem but rather information management, which covered the former. Her projects were continental, building sites in Dubai, purchasing offices in Singapore, design studios in London, and every department was overwhelmed with systems. The finance department was over SAP; the procurement department was over Oracle NetSuite; and a small but growing technology department was currently exploring Odoo as their internal asset management system. All these systems came out with data and each system considered itself as the only source of the truth.

Executive reports sent to the desk of Ms. Patel every week rarely matched the numbers. Unequal exchange rates were represented in project budgets. The Procurement delays issues reported by NetSuite did not match the information in supplier updates via email. The executives wanted one dashboard that would show how the global performance of the ongoing projects was doing. Ms. Patel, who had a more process management background than a technical system background, was faced with a familiar divide the one Sarah, Tom, Emma, and Raj had all encountered. The gulf in between the systems of work and the analysis.

Ms. Patel had her realization moment during one of those extended evening status sessions, as she was scrolling through spreadsheets that were exported out of SAP and a PowerPoint slide of the charts of the finance. We already have data, we are not letting it speak she said, but it is there. The issue was not an end of data--it was its isolation. SAP stored the project actuals as well as purchase order, but without contextual analytics, it looked like an analysis of single brush strokes without the perspective of the full picture. The business intelligence system used in the company, Power BI, was also not utilized and it was waiting to have someone to bridge the two worlds together.

It was that venture which Ms. Patel determined to adopt.

The next day, she met with Mr. Arun who was a quiet systems analyst and years of maintenance of systems integrations of SAP. In case, I can bring live project data into Power BI, Ms. Patel said, can we have real-time performance dashboards? Mr. Arun hesitated. “Technically, yes. Nevertheless, the data provided by SAP can not be easily interpreted. We would need SQL connectors, security access and mapping tables to get a sense of cost centers and WBS elements. Ms. Patel smiled. And now shall we make this a project.

They started with a proof of concept which was a small integration that pulled out data in the SAP Project System (PS) module, and targeted three pilot projects. Mr. Arun created an SQL connector which created a bridge between SAP and the project budgets, project commitments, and actual costs which were all accessible through the database tables of SAP. Ms. Patel formulated questions the dashboards should answer:

with respect to the baseline plans, were we spending on projects as planned? What were the vendors that were making the most delays? Comparison between actual utilization of resources and expectations?

Power BI was made the visualization engine. They were able to create interactive dashboards within days, which showed performance bars that were colored. One click would roll down to the total project expenditure to the purchase orders, vendor category and cost type. What once would have taken hours of manual reconciliation on the spreadsheet was now being displayed in-real-time on the screen. They were so good that when the CFO saw it half in disbelief he said, This is the first time I can see the whole story.

As Ms. Patel realized, what they had accomplished was much more than a technical enhancement it was a cultural overlap between ERP systems and analytics. Over decades, ERP systems were the administrative workhorse of businesses: SAP as the finance system, Oracle NetSuite as the resource planning system, Odoo as the modular operations system. These systems were intended to board, manage as well as standardize transactions. They were strong, and closed. They were not fully capable of their potential until analytics crossed their waters. The combination of ERP and Power BI, or any more contemporary analytics layer is not about creating more visually appealing charts, but changing record-keeping into intelligence.

Within the center of any ERP system is structured data: project, accounts, cost elements, suppliers, assets, and time. The challenge is that this data, though clean and valid, is usually limited to transactional situations. The tables in SAP (including COEP table of cost line items or PRPS table of WBS elements) are designed to be stored and controlled, but not to tell a story. Instead, analytics platforms feed off of narratives, patterns, trends, correlations, anomalies. It is the SQL the bridge that is silent, yet changes inert information into living knowledge.

It did not take long before Ms. Patel came to understand that the integration process was not only the act of connection but also a very deep act of translation. SQL connectors acted as interpreters, and they read SAP tables and transformed them into analytical datasets. Technically, this involved building queries that would retrieve the main fields, project ID, budget amount, actual cost, sponsored spend, and import them into Power BI datasets on a scheduled basis. To a project-management mind, this created more visibility, however.

The initial dashboard that was designed by Ms. Patel was a legend in the firm. A line graph at its top indicated project burn-rate with time. Below was a heat map that showed projects that were more than ten percent above baseline. Three critical metrics that were available in a KPI panel included schedule variance, cost performance index, and resource utilisation rate. All these indicators were directly based on live SAP data. The executives would be able to roll out Power BI on their tablets in meetings and see the real-time performance of the project without asking their manual reports.

ERP systems like SAP and Oracle NetSuite used to be viewed as the repositories of the truth; analytics applications like Power BI convert that truth into understanding. The marriage of the two is not only technical (it is strategic). ERP controls what exists, analytics what it signifies.

However, there were tremendous obstacles associated with the integration process. Enterprise resource planning (ERP) data is inherently complex with every functional module using a unique structural convention namely finance, materials management, human resource etc. The first significant challenge that Priya had to face was when she attempted to match project spending using SAP Controlling (CO) module with timeframes milestones located within Project System. The data fields could not match exactly some of the projects had internal codes not similar across the geographies. She concluded that inconsistency was the major obstacle to analytics, and not technology.

Priya started a data harmonization program to overcome this problem. She worked out a master mapping file that would be a crosswalk between SAP project codes and Power BI identifiers and the nomenclature used internally at the organization. This was painstakingly done but this effort created what she referred to as semantic integrity. As a result, all project identifiers were consolidated into a single reliable key of all datasets. As soon as this foundation was laid down, dashboards obtained a meaningful story.

This impact on the project team was transformational. Site managers, who relied on monthly reports, used daily dashboards to track procurement delays. Finance teams realigned cash flows on a near real-time basis. The vendor managers could identify vendors who were always spending more than budgetary allocations or those who were tardy. The coming together of ERP and analytics had essentially transformed the project office to a dynamically charged command center.

Priya started seeing opportunities that were deeper. Using the capabilities of Power BI in data modeling she was able to report as well as predict performance. She liaised with the analytics department to use predictive models on ERP data. The terminal project costs were projected using historical spending of SAP. The trends of lead-times were analyzed to predict delays in delivery. The dashboards shifted to more predictive (as opposed to merely descriptive) and that indicates the trend of maturation of data-driven project management.

Priya adopted a system of governance as the system developed. The automated nightly data refreshing was done through scheduled SQL tasks. Portfolio-based (engineering, procurement, logistics) and role-based access controls were built in the form of power BI workspaces. This transparency and security coincidence provided that only necessary information was accessed by the executives and the specifics of the operations were protected.

It was followed by the cultural change. Meetings evolved out of deliberation to diagnosis. Teams were focused on remedial actions and root causes instead of questioning data validity. The agenda of the meetings turned out to be the dashboard, the data itself was the discourse. The integration of ERP democratized information and, as a result, hierarchies were eliminated in the favor of shared evidence.

One morning, having a quarterly performance review, Priya presented a dashboard on the comparison of cost performance of all projects throughout the world. One of the red bars caught the attention of the chief financial officer. What is wrong with Project Delta being 12 percent overbudgeted? he inquired. Priya could with one click drill down to vendor-level information. The cost overrun was attributed to the expedited shipping cost in Singapore, the information that was available because of the direct extraction of data in the logistics table of SAP. CFO nodded his head. This is not reporting as such, he said. It is wisdom being given at a thought pace.

Under the refined dashboards, Priya realized that the built system was a new nervous system to the organization- with ERP being the memory and analytics being the conscious interpreter. SAP, Oracle NetSuite and Odoo were offering discipline, standardization and control; Power BI was offering curiosity and interpretation, and foresight. Together, they made projects living things that could sense, learn, and adapt.

This continued into other months where it was integrated. The Oracle NetSuite data was previously independent in the financial system; therefore, an ODBC SQL driver was used to connect it to the same Power BI workspace. It was now possible to cross-reference the vendor invoices in NetSuite with the state of payment in SAP. Open APIs of Odoo allowed them to connect the data of asset-tracking directly to the maintenance dashboards. This was the first time that disparate ERP systems of the organization were harmonized under a unified layer of analytic systems.

The result of this cross-ERP integration was an important implication in project management, which was integrated dashboards of global key performance indicators. Priya came up with a master performance dashboard which showed the cumulative cost variance, schedule adherence and procurement efficiency at all the regions. All KPIs could be traced to the transaction that gave rise to them in the respective ERP system, thus, holding them accountable. In the event that one figure seemed to be suspicious, any user could look at the source of such a figure with a single click- a feature that Priya described as trust traceability.

These dashboards became part of the morning briefing ritual by the executive team. The Power BI application would be introduced by the chief executive officer before the daily operations call. Dashboards had grown to be more than measurement devices and became management tools.

One of the most powerful insights was obtained after the correlation between the procurement lead times obtained in

NetSuite and the data on the project delays received in SAP. The analysis showed that projects with a mean supplier delay of greater than seven days were more likely to miss milestone deadlines by twice. With this information, procurement policies have been changed, and preferred supplier contracts have been renegotiated. On-time delivery of projects grew by 14 within a quarter. The information did not only shed light on a problem, but it also brought about behavioral modification.

The deeper Priya interacted the more it became clear that ERP analytics integration was transforming project management. It was no longer enough to only measure cost, schedule and scope but new measurements included data freshness, dashboard adoption and insight latency; interval between an event and its recognition. Previously serving as a rear-view mirror of the organization, analytics integration has turned the ERP systems into a windshield.

Nevertheless, Priya made sure that she did not romanticize technology. One of thc intcgration sprouts experienced an SQL connector failure mid-way which caused data refresh errors that introduced false data to executive dashboards. The episode was a wake-up call that data governance is not a one time achievement but a discipline. As a result, she introduced automated validation checks so that every night load of data was compared with the number of transactions in SAP and only validated data was published to Power BI.

This quality control was efficient. At the time when the next external audit was done, the auditors noted that the project performance dashboards resembled underlying financials more than similar dashboards in most of the firms that they have audited. The reason behind this was straightforward: all the metrics were pegged to ERP data, which is the most authoritative data that can be obtained.

The philosophical impact of integration was in addition to the technical success. The team that Priya was in started seeing ERP data not as a record, but as a story that is being narrated now. An increase in the number of purchase orders was not just a number, it was a wave of action, a sign of movement or pressure. A decreasing cost performance index was not only red: it was an indication that something had to be investigated. ERP data, which was formerly bureaucratic, was turned into a story.

At the year-end, the Power BI environment created by Priya had more than a hundred reports and dashboards with each being connected to live ERP data using SQL connectors. But the greatest outcome was neither the dashboards themselves but the behavioural change that they brought about. Evidence-based decision-making took place. Projections were made data-driven. Teams were starting to view data as a common language that was not geographical or departmental.

The leadership team at Priya noticed that the accuracy of forecasting was also enhanced by the integration. The predictive models of cost estimation of projects at the firm became more accurate using ERP data. The machine-learning capabilities of Power BI helped them to spot any outlier on cost trends. There was one case where a model overran a significant infrastructure project in Dubai by 8% in two months with regard to its material cost base. The timely notification enabled the procurement to renegotiate supplier terms which saved the company almost half a million dollars.

These examples reinforced the reputation of ERP systems that are integrated with analytics as not being functional devices but strategic resources. They are the silent drivers of competitive advantage. It was best defined by Priya in her quarterly report, that is: ERP records what happened. Analytics is simply a description of why and what we should do next.

The company standardized the practice shortly. Every new project charter now had an obligatory ERP analytics strategy, outlining the modules that would provide data, the method of defining KPIs and the establishment of dashboards to be overseen by the executives. It was no longer considered that the success of a project was determined by the deliverables or budgets but also by the honesty and thoughtfulness of the data ecosystem.

The experiment of Priya was adopted as the institutional policy.

Her position as the system matured became one not of project manager, but of the one colleagues jokingly referred to as Chief Translator as she was in between the systems, analytics and strategy. She did not have to spend much time counting and rather to analyze numbers. Executives needed to expand their geographical areas; they resorted to her dashboards to find evidence on her feasibility. Teams sought budget changes that they supported using live ERP analytics. The reactive decisions were changed to anticipatory ones.

The further connection with Power BI also made cross-domain analytics available. Priya used correlations of workforce utilisation and project performance by linking HR data, provided by SAP SuccessFactors. She found that work-balanced teams were neither overworked nor idle, and therefore, best in schedule compliance. The observation inspired a new resourcing approach: the redistribution of the workloads every week according to the dashboard indicators. Project overruns were reduced significantly within the next three months.

ERP systems that could have been regarded as administrative liabilities had turned out to be empowerment sources. The project managers were no longer plan operators but pattern steerers.

When thinking about the transformation, Priya usually explained the integration humanly. It is the heartbeat of an organisation so is an ERP system, she told the group of management trainees. It monitors all Pulses- all the transactions, all the expenses, all the deliveries. But we do not know, unless we have analytics, that the heart beats. We are not aware of its healthiness. Power BI is the stethoscope, it allows us to hear, judge, and act.

Her analogy resonated. The interface she created was not a technical interface but a cognitive interface a means of enabling the organisation to think in real time. The dashboards were not reflective: they were tools of recognition.

The case of Priya highlights the extended functions of the ERP systems in the era of analytics. SAP, Oracle NetSuite, and Odoo are not single line software collections, they are the backbones of modern companies. They are not powerful in terms of storing data, but in terms of the intelligent usage of the data. Combined with visualization software like Power BI, they can be the canvas on which the performance, risks, and opportunities of the project are painted in a very vivid manner.

Considering the project-management perspective, the moral of the story is obvious: ERP reports are not administrative artefacts but rather strategic tools. They are the beat of the progress, and a timely status update can adjust the operational detail to the strategic direction. Dashboards that are driven by the ERP data converts abstract KPIs to action narratives.

To Priya, every dashboard was a subject of discussion. She would have to spend hours collecting updates and then she can open Power BI and tell, Here is what the data is telling us today. It was a transition between describing the past to dealing with the present- and creating the future.

Priya looked at the master dashboard once more as she was going to conduct another board meeting towards the end of the fiscal year. A mosaic of green indicators was shown on the screen costs within tolerance, schedules on track, vendor performance improving. To the right hand side there was a small amber alert that there might be a delay in supply of materials in Jakarta. A few clicks made her recognize the supplier, look at the purchase-order information and give an alert to the logistics team before the problem could go out of proportion.

This, she imagined, is what integration really is: not merely the communication, but the collaboration that people work together.

This meeting started with the Chief Executive Officer asking about the health of the project. Priya displayed the dashboard to the main screen. She said that our ERP systems are no longer databases. “They are narrative tools. All the numbers shown here are based directly on the work done by our teams on the ground sources around the world- night-to-night, tested and quoted in governance and brought out in a form easy to follow. We are able not only to see what is happening but also the motives behind the scenes-and what needs to be done next.

This was followed by a moment of silence when the display was digested by the executives. The technology did not impress them but rather its coherence. This is the first time that all projects, all regions, all functions were in touch with each other via one single truth.

ERP systems have always been the basis of the management of the enterprise. Priya has transformed that base into a window through analytics integration, a tool of observation, understanding, and leadership.

After the meeting was over, she started to think about the times when SAP reports and Power BI charts seemed to belong to different worlds. In the current day, they constitute two parts of the same vision, data and decision, logic and leadership, system and narrative.

That is the context behind the existence of data-driven project management: that any data, no matter how complex, simply awaits a listening ear to discern its story; and to do something about it.

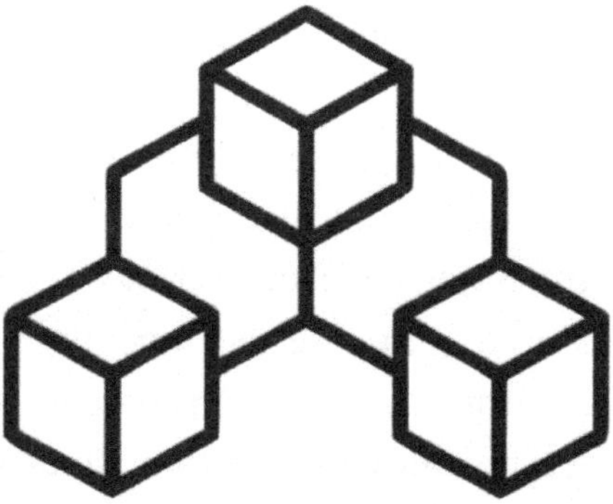

CHAPTER 8

BLOCKCHAIN FOR DATA INTEGRITY IN ANALYTICS

From Fragile Trust to Immutable Truth: Alex's Story

At the time Alex Verma had joined the fintech startup in early 2025, he felt that his ten years of experience leading digital transformation initiatives had prepared him to deal with any responsibility. He had managed to conduct cloud migrations, define agile structures and organize cross-time zone teams. However, he could not predict the insidious, non-obvious corruption in the form of which he received the message on one of Tuesday mornings, which could make the investors lose their trust in the financial analytics of the company.

The startup was focused on digital lending, which collected loan data of hundreds of microfinance partners. Its platform transacted thousands of deals, including disbursals, repayments, interest earnings, and credit risk adjustments, every day. These records were fed into the analytics engine where they generated dashboards to investors and regulators. Under an audit, there were differences between reported figures and underlying raw transactions. It was not fraud; it was drift. There must have been minor inconsistencies between data entry and data ETL pipelines and reporting levels.

These differences seemed inconsequential to the naked eye, a few hundred dollars out of millions every day of dealings. Nonetheless, fintech is sacrosanct in terms of precision. According to the CFO, it is a trust fracture. Unless data-driven analytics could be assured to communicate unchangeable fact, then everything derived on them, whether predictive analytics or dashboards, was just sand-castled.

Data governance protocols and audit trails could only suppress, not remove such risk as realised by Alex. Not just compliance was needed by the company, as it needed immutability, a record that could not be modified or altered retrospectively, regardless of whether it was a system error or intentional.

As a result, he suggested a concept that will change the data architecture of the organisation: blockchain integration as the basis of analytical integrity.

The idea gave rise to curiosity and skepticism at the same time. Blockchain is linked with the concept of cryptocurrencies and speculative markets, which is associated by the vast majority of people. But Alex did not suggest a crypto coin, he suggested a book of truth. Take this into consideration, he told the leadership. We rely on financial data integrity in our analytics. Blockchain is not a technology that involves money storage, but rather one that involves trust maintenance. It makes sure that all the transactions that we are analyzing are verifiable, auditable and cannot be tampered with.

The executives were paying closer attention. The CTO raised an eyebrow. That is to write off our transaction logs to a blockchain, suggested you? he replied.

"Precisely," Alex replied. Our use of blockchain is not going to be used as a payment, but as a proof.

He formed a small task force, consisting of data engineers, security experts and analysts to prototype what he called the Immutable Data Pipeline. It would not substitute the current databases and analytics engines of the company, but would run concurrently. Each financial operation going into the analytics system would be hashed or a cryptographic fingerprint generated via SHA- 256 and the fingerprint would be recorded in a private blockchain network operating under Hyperledger Fabric.

The blocks would signify a batch of transactions per day, which is timestamped, cryptographically signed, and digitally attached to the previous block. In case any record in the analytics pipeline is changed, whether by mistake or not, the hash comparison would fail, which would immediately indicate the tampering of the data.

The further Alex then explained, the more the vision grew clearer: blockchain as the layer of integrity of analytics.

The implementation was done slowly. The pilot phase was focused on one use case: verifying the Daily repayment data of partner institutions. This data was normally posted through APIs, cleaned in SQL databases and then visualised in Power BI dashboards to executives. A new checkpoint was added in this flow by the team of Alex a special blockchain validation node.

Every time the API received repayment information, the system hashed every transaction and stored it on Hyperledger blockchain. This was later on when the analytics engine was asked to report on the data, it hashed the transactions again and compared it to the blockchain entries. In case one of the numbers would have been changed, say, a payment of 1000 dollars registered as 1010, the difference would have been noted.

The team initially tested the system using dummy data, corruption of records in the middle-of the pipeline. The blockchain has instantly identified the anomalies. This, observed the data engineer, is comparable to the placement of a digital notary stamp on each transaction.

The achievement of the pilot triggered the expansion of the possibilities. They then expanded the validation system to other important data sets, interest calculations, customer risk scores and regulatory filings. What it produced was a self-auditing data ecosystem where analytics were regularly checked against an unalterable ledger.

Alex also changed his dashboards. A small green lock icon was located next to every key performance indicator. When it hovered it gave the message: Data Verified through Blockchain-No Integrity Violation was detected. Even though this cue is visually simple, it bore a deep psychological impact; executives have come to believe in dashboards not only to be insightful but genuine.

With the increase of the scale of integration, Alex proposed a second level of blockchain with the use of Ethereum smart contracts to provide inter-party transparency. However, whereas Hyperledger ensured internal integrity, Ethereum had a decentralised structure, allowing external regulators and partner institutions to check the authenticity of transactions on their own. Permissioned access would help regulators to ensure that all loans reported on compliance filings had an equivalent blockchain-supported record.

The two-chain system Hyperledger due to control by two, Ethereum to selective verification by the general population, became a strong example of a hybrid blockchain design. Factually, the fintech company has created a provable gap between analytics and audit, between quantitative measurement and truth.

The project looked at through the prism of project-management was an eye-opener. Implementing blockchains was not just a technical implementation, but a cultural change to radical transparency. Alex met opposition in groups that had reservations about complexity. What is the point of an extra layer, some asked. We have already secured our databases.

He clarified the concept using analogy. Blockchain is safer against internal users who may quietly change the historical records, as opposed to traditional security measures that guard against external intrusions. This utterance was heavily felt in a time when trust had not only been a company asset but a company liability.

Blockchain transformed the understanding of the governance of data. It ceased to be a peripheral issue or a box to be filled on compliance but was a part of project architecture. In each analytics project, Alex established a separate workstream named Integrity validation, the product of which included cryptographic audits and implementation of blockchain nodes and hash comparison testing. What used to be regarded as, exotic practices transformed to become standard practices.

The impact on organizational confidence became palpable as time passed by weeks to months. Internal auditors cut verification loops by three quarters. The regulatory submissions received less inquiries. The Chief Financial Officer who had earlier on raised the issue of data drift commented to Alex, our numbers now have veracity attached to them.

Outside the financial technology industry, Alex started to identify the wider implication of connecting blockchain to analytics. He joined forces with a logistics company to test blockchain in supply chain analytics, an area that has an infamous record of disjointed data. There was a lot of delays in shipments, invoices, and records on customs since the stakeholders were using different systems. Using the blockchain approach to shipment, each scan, handoff, or invoice is timestamped and hashed, placing any party in a synchronized and verifiable history.

This data was represented in power BI dashboards, which allowed project managers to track the lifecycle of a product, starting with the manufacturer and continuing with the retailer, that relies on this blockchain. The problem of late deliveries can be identified with an indisputable evidence. Measures of supplier performance proved beyond doubt. The system has not only made them more efficient but also removed conflicts based on the he said she said data discrepancies.

Alex also realized that the real value of blockchain was not technical, but rather epistemological in nature, and it changed the way organizations perceived their data. Trust in a traditional system was based on reputation, access or documentation. Trust in a blockchain-based system is algorithmic, and it is a part of cryptographic consensus.

This was a very minor, but significant difference that repackaged the risk approach among project managers. Over decades, risk management was a matter in which the emphasis has been on uncertainty, which is what may fail to occur in the future. The concept of blockchain brought a new aspect: the security of the past. A transaction having become recorded and verified was closed forever. This time confidence provided a background on which analytics could be set without falling over.

In a world fintech event, Alex introduced his firm as the developer of the Immutable Analytics Framework. Onstage, he described how blockchain formed the basis of data transparency: Analytics informs us of what has already taken place; predictive models of what might take place. However, blockchain opens the eyes on what is undeniable. It is the magnet that keeps us on track so that all the knowledge we come up with is pegged on truth.

The demonstration was of popular concern. The players in the industry already saw other uses outside of the financial sector; health records, environmental surveillance, digital identity, and even academic credentials checking. Blockchain could present unquestionable assurance wherever there was a concern on data integrity.

In the case of Alex, the essence was practical, though--based on verifiable fact. The main obstacle, he warned, was in striking a balance. He said, Powerful as blockchain can be, it must not be used to serve complexity, but to serve clarity. The task is never to transform all the data sets into a line of blocks, but to protect the data, the integrity of which is the foundation of our credibility.

The changing maturity of the technology was captured in his words. Blockchain is no panacea; it is a fine tool that should be used where verification is a matter of life and death.

Tools, Techniques, and Project Management Insight

Technically, the framework designed by Alex was based on two foundations Hyperledger Fabric and Ethereum Smart Contracts that fulfilled two different requirements of the analytics integrity. Hyperledger had a permissioned control, which was the best in the context of the enterprise, where access levels and participants were pre-determined. It gave the fintech team the ability to have special project-specific channels in order to keep a secret of sensitive financial information without losing out on blockchain immutability.

Ethernet, however, provided programmability. Alex used smart contracts to automate the validation of data across institutional borders. To provide an example, whenever a new set of transactions was hashed and stored on-chain, a smart contract notified the interested parties and auditors automatically. This automation was used to substitute manual reporting which was tedious with cryptographically verified events.

The technical workflow was manuscript sophistication simple:

1. Transaction Ingestion: APIs or database updates were used to enter data into the system.

2. Generation of Hash: Every transaction or data set was transformed into a cryptographic hash.

3. Blockchain Recording: The metadata, hash and time were recorded in a block.

4. Verification Layer: The data retrieved by analytics systems were rehashed against on-chain hashes.

5. Visualization: Dashboards were also used to present metrics as well as indicators of integrity status.

This pipeline was a technical one, but it served as a prototype on the data assurance in various projects. All KPI in power BI had been supported by a blockchain signature thereby rendering analytics as credible as certified financial statements.

Alex applied the same principle in the case of the supply chain. The modular architecture of Hyperledger enabled individual nodes to be run by each of the logistics partners manufacturers, distributors, and transporters. Upon a shipment event, it was placed into the blockchain, creating a common record that can be seen by any party involved. When analysts made performance reports, both classic databases and the blockchain were asked by Power BI and uniformity was confirmed before visualising insights were provided.

These integrations demonstrated a wider fact: blockchain did not displace analytics - it strengthened it. Technically, it was not a source of data but a data verifier. Philosophically, it transferred the notion of trust to a property.

This change had significant implications to project managers. Categories that were traditionally included in risk registers were cost, schedule, scope, and compliance. Data Integrity Risk is a new category that Alex included after adoption of blockchain. It measured the probability and the effects of data tampering or corruption on a decision made. Blockchain emerged the mitigation strategy- engineered solution to an epistemic problem.

Alex redefined the major questions in project governance meetings. Teams did not inquire whether the data is accurate; they inquired whether they could prove that it is. The difference distorted responsibility. The validation of the data shifted towards verification after the analysis to embedded validation.

To apply the concept of blockchain in a lifecycle of a project, Alex formulated five principles:

1. Begin with Purpose: Determine what data really needs to be immutable. Excessive use results in bloat; discriminating use maintains productivity.

2. Design to Auditability: Cause the blockchain records to be connected to analytical datasets by unique identifiers.

3. Automise Verification: Compare hash values from scripts and smart contracts.

4. Be transparent but not open: Select permissioned ledgers in sensitive areas to achieve transparency and privacy.

5. Train Stakeholders: Data integrity is not a technical skill, it is a human skill as well; and teams should know why blockchain is important.

Such principles transformed blockchain into a buzzword to a tool of governance.

In the course of time Alex observed the surprising phenomenon. The existence of verification based on blockchain changed the behaviour of teams. More discipline in data entry came about. The analysts verified inputs twice before submission as they knew they would be cryptographically stamped. Effectually, blockchain did not only ensure the safety of data; it enhanced data culture.

This was also observed by the investors of the company. The increased credibility passed on to quarterly reports (now labeled Verified by Blockchain) was higher. Regulatory authorities commended the initiative of the firm as far as data transparency is concerned. Rival companies started looking into similar architectures. What began as a minor risk reduction measure was now an opportunity of differentiation.

Blockchain provided a contribution to analytics more than security, but it offered a new facet of transparency coupled with accountability. Each data point had lineage. Each metric had proof.

The project management lessons were obvious. In a world that was becoming more and more analytics controlled, trust became the new currency. And blockchain, implemented wisely, was the mint.

The last project retrospective by Alex reflected his overall experience:

We used to have analytics that was a mirror of data; it has become a mirror of truth. Blockchain did not increase our figures or their beauty, it made them authentic. And in finance, and that is all.

During the following years, the Immutable Analytics Framework created by Alex turned into an example of data-driven governance. It was used in business schools as a model of how technology could not only fix technical issues but transform the philosophy of management.

Blockchain was already in the business lexicon not as a technology of the future but as a pragmatic norm a silent incorruptible observer of the account of data.

And in all the dashboards where the green verification lock was displayed, Alex was not only able to see numbers but integrity itself, conserved, demonstrable and eternal.

CHAPTER 9

AI AND MACHINE LEARNING IN PROJECT ANALYTICS

Sofia's Experiment: Turning Data into Foresight

Once Sofia Mendes became a portfolio manager of a global construction and infrastructure consortium, she entered a world of constant multi-tasking. There were twenty-seven ongoing projects that were scattered in three different continents and they competed over the same limited supply of engineers, designers, procurement specialists and field teams. The heads of different departments would argue over the same human and material resources every week. Any given project needed one more structural engineer or two more welders.

Who was the one, who saw this was not a problem of schedules, but an optimization problem, and was an pragmatic project manager with some experience in data analytics? The spreadsheets that she had inherited before her were failing to carry the complexity burden. The ERP dashboards of the firm even connected to SAP and Power BI could not provide an answer to the question that appears every Monday morning to her: What is the best way to use our resources in our portfolio that would allow us to get the maximum value out of them without overworking our teams?

This was a misleadingly easy question mathematically impossible. It meant the ability to forecast work loads, skills needed, project dependencies, and risk factors- in actual time. Sofia understood that the dynamic interaction of variables in a portfolio could not be followed by the intuition of any human, regardless of his experience. She required something smarter, a system, which was able to learn through patterns and forecast the results.

This problem was solved during an interview with Arjun, a data scientist in the analytics department of the company. During one afternoon when we had coffee together, he described how project behavior could be modeled with machine learning. He explained that it was possible to train an algorithm to identify which mixes of skills, project phases, and workloads resulted in delays or cost overruns. It can then suggest the best resource allocations in accordance with the past success trends.

Sofia's eyes lit up. This is why you are telling me the system can learn how to better manage the resources than we do?

she said. "Not better," Arjun replied. Quick--and more regularly.

In a few weeks, they rolled out a pilot program, Project Atlas, to implement artificial intelligence in the allocation of resources to its portfolio. The concept was not that complex and yet groundbreaking: input all the accessible historical project information into the engine (scheduling, budgeting, resource records, task execution, and performance indicators), and leave it to the system to find some latent relationships between resource allocation and project achievement.

To start with, they have combined information across several sources: ERP modules to obtain staffing data, project managers to receive project timelines, and analytics dashboard to obtain performance metrics. Sofia made sure that the information of each project contained the attributes that were important such as team size, skills composition, time frame, cost and results. This was made the training dataset.

Arjun described the rationale to the bigger team: AI, on the most basic level, is pattern recognition. The structure of data, which is clustered, correlates, depends on human beings, machine learning models reveal. After training, they are able to foresee the desired result of which configuration of inputs will give desired results.

The model that they initially implemented was a clustering algorithm, which was aimed at clustering projects on the basis of similarity in terms of complexity, skill mix and length. Applying unsupervised learning, the algorithm found out that successful projects had a few things in common:

equal diversity of skills, constant resource turnover, average workload fluctuations. Projects with poor performances, on the contrary, had irregular staffing patterns and unbalanced tasks distribution.

Sofia saw the potential. The system would suggest the way to organize the teams of future projects based on identifying groups of successful patterns. She said in a leadership review that it is the equivalent of a knowledgeable portfolio manager coded into the algorithm.

They then followed it up with an implementation of a classification model which is a supervised learning model to find out whether a new project would have resource related delays. Historical data was labeled as being on-time or delayed and the model was trained using input features including the amount of active engineers during a given phase, average skill overlap, and variance in project duration.

No one could have predicted the predictions to be accurate. In the original version, the model was above 85% accurate in predicting projects that would have staffing problems. More significantly, it offered interpretability with the feature-importance analysis meaning which variables had the strongest impact.

As an example, the model has shown that projects whose cross-team dependency is more than 20 percent on average had three times higher probabilities of delay compared to projects with a lower dependency. This one observation prompted Sofia to restructure operations by cutting off dependency chains whereby key disciplines had to finish their design cycles prior to handover. The increase was instantaneous.

Following this initial success, Sofia and Arjun created a recommendation system a recommendation system an AI-based decision support system that proposed the best distribution of resources to be used in the projects. This model used the principles of reinforcement learning and kept its recommendations improving according to the results, which were observed in the real world. When a suggested allocation of resources had raised the performance, the algorithm solidified that pattern of decisions; otherwise, it modified.

Throughout the mid-year, Project Atlas had developed into a smart co-pilot to the project management office. Nowadays, every morning when Sofia opened her dashboard, she did not see any static report. Rather, she considered predictions, which are identifying projects that are at risk, teams that are not fully utilized, and how the re-allocation of the two engineers in Project Delta to Project Orion would impact the performance of the whole portfolio.

It is not analytics, she told her staff. “It is foresight at scale.”

The change spread throughout the company. Resource meetings became less of a debate and more an evidence based deliberation. When the department heads started relying on the recommendations on the system, it was based on facts and proven by results. As the time passed, Sofia could trace a quantifiable improvement: the total number of project delays decreased by 17%, utilization performance grew by almost 22%.

AI had not taken her position away, it had increased her decision-making ability. Still, Sofia was also keen to stress the idea that AI models did not act as oracles but as tools. Combine data and assumptions with which we feed them, she reminded her team, are only as good as the data we give them. It is not to mechanize judgment, but to make it informed.

She was able to take a balanced view-point that made the endeavor sustainable. When the executives later asked her about applying artificial intelligence to other functions, including procurement forecasting, risk prediction, and even maintenance planning, Sofia insisted on the use of an algorithm with a human-in-the-loop validation process. This was not the aim of blind automation but symbiotic intelligence. Arjun had been working on a prototype of a basic neural network to increase the accuracy of predictions in resource allocation behind the scenes. He built it with one of the most popular deep-learning frameworks known as TensorFlow. In order to achieve standardization of inputs, he used StandardScaler of scikit-learn to normalize the features like team size, duration and cost variance. The architecture of the model was also designed to be lightweight, having just a handful of dense layers, to be illustrative of the idea.

The simplified pseudocode looked like this:

```
import tensorflow as tf

from sklearn.preprocessing import StandardScaler


# Assume X = project features, y = performance score
```

```
scaler = StandardScaler()
X_scaled = scaler.fit_transform(X)

model = tf.keras.Sequential([
    tf.keras.layers.Dense(64, activation='relu', input_shape=(X.shape[1],)),
    tf.keras.layers.Dense(1)
])

model.compile(optimizer='adam', loss='mse')
model.fit(X_scaled, y, epochs=10)
```

This fundamental neural network was trained on the scores of project performance according to historical patterns of resource allocation. This practically translated to the fact that the system would be able to model various staffing scenarios and predict their probable effect before implementation.

Sofia was intrigued by the ability of a small piece of code to convert data into useful forecasts. After the model had been trained and fine-tuned, it started suggesting almost optimal team formations on new projects. It updated weights in real-time, thus creating a living learning system by evolving with each new dataset update.

To implement the model, Arjun applied it to Google Cloud AI platform, which allowed Arjun to scale it seamlessly and integrate it with the current analytics processes. The model was trained in the night with the help of the GPU resources and every morning it offered updated predictions to the

Power BI dashboards. At the same time, they experimented with Azure Machine Learning and used it to autodeploy pipelines, test pipeline orchestration, retraining triggers, and model version control.

It was these tools that allowed machine learning not to exist as an experiment but as a part of the wider data architecture of the company.

The system became mature and Sofia found herself in other dimensions of governance of projects. Artificial intelligence had not only brought opportunity, but responsibility. She worked collaboratively with the ethics committee in order to have transparency of the algorithm- parameters and assumptions of the model are available to audit. Unless we want to leave machines, she said, to make such decisions as would influence the workload and stress level of people, we should ask them to be clear.

Her demand to promote transparency was an AI governance pillar in the organization. A Model Fact Sheet where the training data, accuracy data, possible biases, and retraining timelines were documented was required with each model deployment. This habit brought about accountability and trust among the departments.

The development of a so-called feedback ecosystem was among the most important consequences of Project Atlas. All model predictions (that is, risk, delay, and resource optimisation) were oriented to the real results. The variance was logarithmic and the system acquired knowledge at a time. The AI was no longer a predictive engine, but an adaptive partner, the knowledge of which was improved at each project cycle.

In a review of global project portfolio, Sofia gave out the cumulative results. We wanted to do away with passive allocation and start optimisation, she informed the board. Just that has been attained with machine learning. We no longer conjecture, we feign. We will not react any more--we expect it.

The CFO inquired whether such models were capable of determining the future workforce requirements. Sofia nodded. “Yes. The algorithms used to predict the delay of a project can be used to predict a talent shortage. When we are aware of the skills that are overutilised in the present time, then we could recruit six months ahead.

The wisdom was close to the heart. What started out as a tactic experiment that seeks to optimise resources has now become a tool of strategic planning. It is now dealing with its human capital as an optimisable, analysable system, which is not dehumanised. The models never substitute human judgment, they refine it.

The process codified by Sofia in a project management framework was called AI-Augmented Portfolio Governance. It outlines the stages data preparation, model selection, validation, deployment, and monitoring and resembles the standard project lifecycles except with AI checks. To ensure that data are sufficient to drive machine-learning-driven insights, every project charter currently contains a section, namely Predictive Readiness Assessment.

The introduction of AI in project analytics has turned into corporate DNA.

The Intelligence Management: Project Insight and Future.

The trip of Sofia shed light on more than technical skills it was a discovery of the new philosophy of intelligent project management. Artificial intelligence and machine learning is not only a speed or efficiency tool, it is an accelerator of new approaches of comprehending complexity. Whereas conventional analytics explain the past, AI explains the present and predicts the future.

The project office has become functional on three dimensional analysis dimensions:

1. Descriptive Analytics What happened? (ERP dashboards and reports)

2. Predictive Analytics What will probably occur? These are (Machine-learn models and simulations).

3. Prescriptive Analytics- What are we to do about it? (AI-driven recommendations)

These layers are combined to create a range of understanding, turning project information into an inert document to a flexible tool of vision.

Nonetheless, the path is not smooth sailing. The adoption of AI in work processes of projects requires new literacy patterns. The project manager should also ensure that he or she gathers enough knowledge about the algorithms to understand their results critically. Analysts should develop sufficient knowledge about projects in order to put their models into perspective. What the unification of these fields has produced is a new hybrid role of the analytics-fluent project leader.

This became a self-imposed mission of Sofia. She held cross-training classes in which project managers got to understand how to read confusion matrices and regression plots but data scientists got to understand Gantt chart and stakeholder matrices. The outcome was a common understanding between human reason and machine reasoning- common language.

Technically, the next step that Sofia is going to undertake is that of model generalisation. The existing models of machine-learning are very useful in the company portfolio and restricted in the new types of projects or regions. To mitigate this, Arjun investigated transfer learning a method in which a previously trained model transforms to new data with minimal retraining. The AI implementation would be able to make use of world project trends but provide local suggestions by using this approach.

The vision is ambitious: it aims to develop the AI engine that would perceive project management as its own dynamic system and learns about it through architecture projects in Dubai, manufacturing projects in Singapore, and infrastructure projects in Europe, and then generalises its learnings into generalised insights.

Sofia was practical but idealistic. She told a conference audience later in the same year that Artificial Intelligence will not make project management useless. It will make it more human-like because it will put us free of mechanical decisions and focus on creative ones.

She emphasized how AI contributed to eliminating one of the oldest dilemmas in project management the efficiency versus empathy one. AI reduced overwork and burnout by maximizing the use of resources. It was able to counter this by forecasting risks before they materialized and thus avoiding the crisis management the norm.

Her leadership saw the company start implementing AI preparedness in its project schedules. Certain milestones were now taken into consideration in the planning stage:

- Data Collection Window - setting up of data sets needed to model.

- Sprint- Model Development It occurs during parallel phases to design or initiation.

- Validation and Tuning Cycle -by making sure there are performance thresholds.

- Deployment and Monitoring- aligning model rollouts and project execution.

This assimilation raised AI development to become a first-class citizen in project lifecycles and no longer an afterthought. The company came to call them intelligent timelines schedules that took into consideration the evolution of more than the deliverables but the intelligence that determined the schedule.

With time, Sofia also noticed that AI affected the decision cadence in the organization. Teams did not wait until the end of the phase, but responded to predictive warnings every minute. The decision-making rhythm turned into agile, adaptive, and evidence-based.

Her last thought in the Project Atlas Report was a concise wrap-up of the change:

Project management cannot be the future of Artificial Intelligence, but the conscience of data. It takes lessons out of our past in order to guide us behave wisely today. It combines uncertainty with human judgment, making it strategy.

The effectiveness of the experiment carried out by Sofia reverberated in the industries. What started as a neural network forecasting resource performance turned out to be a model of implementing AI to all strata of enterprise analytics.

Google Cloud AI and Azure ML were still the main drivers behind their predictive pipelines, though it is not the tools that have brought value to them, it is the mindset. Teams of Sofia were trained to think as an algorithm but to be empathetic, which proves that the optimal application of artificial intelligence is to augment human intelligence.

By the end of the year, when she went through the portfolio dashboard of the company (which was now filled with adaptive predictions and AI-generated insights), Sofia smiled. It was the first occasion in her career whereby she did not need to make assumptions on where the next resource bottleneck would arise. The system already knew.

And as a project manager that was a revolution, indeed.

CHAPTER 10

FINTECH MEETS DATA ANALYTICS

James was tying his tie and staring at the giant monitor in the conference room of the young fintech startup FinSphere Technologies, located in the middle of the financial sector of London. The screen was lit with dashboards - charts, churn graphs and customer segments that were flashing in real time. James was in the company just eighteen months and during this time he had witnessed a reoccurring problem which no one could be heard to correct. As new users were pouring, retention rates continued to drop. Thousands of people registered every month, spent several days using the app and disappeared. The marketing campaigns were adjusted, the customer scripts were re-written, and customer loyalty bonuses were tested. But the churn curve was intractably high.

James was not supposed to be a data scientist as a project manager. He had to do this to make sure that the implementation of new features was uninterrupted, the coordination of cross-functional teams, and that projects are not derailed after losing track of the business objectives. At one place of work where management was boasting of making all decisions based on data, he frequently felt that data was speaking to him in a language he did not quite comprehend. Numbers were all about, and little sense. He made a joke that dashboards were drowning and the company was starving of insight.

On one of his late nights, when examining log customer-feedback, he saw something. Some of the users complained that there was too much delay in the process of transaction-verification at the peak hours. Others were also trying to complain being locked out of accounts after numerous incorrect logins which the system counted as suspicious activity. The pattern was not apparent on the dashboard, but it was there in the words - covert to the eye. James started questioning the analytics team, which was hidden behind the graphs and metrics, whether it missed the human touch behind the figures.

The following day, he came in to the analytics department in a purposeful manner. The data analyst in charge (Clara) was up to her knees in SQL queries. In my opinion, I believe that we are losing customers not due to the fact that they are not interested in the product, but due to the fact that we are marking as a potential fraud, the legitimate users of the product, James, said. They are becoming restless and quitting. Clara leaned back. Interesting supposition, she said. "Let's test it." That was the first sentence of a project that would transform the customer strategy of FinSphere. They agreed to develop a predictive analytics model to know the customer-churn behavior. It was not concerning who was leaving but why they were leaving.

They began with the fundamentals: integration of data. The customer information of FinSphere was distributed among various systems. The CRM had the profile of demographic and engagement record. The financial database contained transaction history, risk rating and activities of the accounts. The customer-service portal monitored customer complains, responsiveness of tickets and customer satisfaction questionnaires. All these systems were not talking to one another. James recalled previous sections of his own experience, when miscellaneous information had wrecked projects, and he was not going to have that repeated.

They developed integrated view with the help of the IT team Python scripts and SQL connectors. CRM data was imported into a staging database on a nightly basis and was cleansed, standardized and compared with financial transactions by unique customer IDs. Power BI dashboards have been created to show patterns in the areas of engagement, transaction behavior, and frequency of complaints. FinSphere would be experiencing a single customer experience, the first ever, since it was founded, sign-up to exit.

In days, the revelations started appearing. Multiple flagged customers were five times more likely to close their accounts in the course of a week, regardless of whether the transactions were legitimate or not. The affected people usually had low average balances but high frequency of transactions - sign of active and loyal customers. The platform fraud-detection algorithms, which were intended to safeguard the platform, were unwillingly pushing away their most active consumers.

This vindicated and alarmed James. Its fraud detection system is based on strict rule logic, which was flagging real customers as suspicious because of similar activity patterns, which was automated. The irony was torturous, analytics that were supposed to protect the business was turning into a bane to its expansion.

The second stage of the project was the implementation of predictive analytics. Clara created a churn-prediction model in Scikit-learn, which is a Python library. They trained it to use historical data, and the variables represented in the historical data were: the delay in transactions, failed logins, interaction with customer support and the risk score. The accuracy of the model increased with time to a cross-validation of 87 percent. It was also obvious that churn was not accidental but predictable.

James did not start off with technicalities when presenting the model to the executive team. He began with a case story a real customer who had walked out out of getting a false flag. Next was the numbers, which demonstrated that in the event that they were capable of decreasing false fraud flags by 10 per cent, retention would grow by 15 per cent, the equivalent to an extra £1.2m of revenue per year. The dashboards were no longer meaningless. The executives bent over and no longer viewed data as an abstract concept, but as a lifeline to growth.

Fintech analytics had always been characterized by fraud detection. The industry trusted the highly developed models that identify the aberrant transactions and eliminate financial crime. However, what James and Clara found out was that there was a fine line between security and user experience. Inadequate fraud controls put the company at risk, excessive one produced tension and drove off honest patrons. This is where data analytics needed to develop, but it would not be a crude implement but an elegant decision-making tool.

Within the next few months, the analytics model was made a part of the operational systems. Risk scores in SQL were re-calibrated to factor-in behavioral information in CRM. Churn probability and transaction risk were now available in Power BI dashboards, and teams could make choices based on them. In the event that the behavior of the customer caused an alarm as a result of fraud, but at the same time was characterized by high activity and positive service contact, the system will be marked to be reviewed manually instead of being restricted in the first place. The ratio of the fraud to the churn in the company was reduced drastically and customer satisfaction ratings increased.

James soon set another challenge, namely how to make analytics practical under regulatory regulations. The models in the fintech sector are required to comply with rigorous laws including the PSD2, GDPR, and local AML laws. Predictive analytics is effective alone, yet it is not effective on its own. All the model parameters and data fields should be traceable, explainable and auditable.

During one compliance review, an auditor inquired, one morning, how the churn prediction model works. James smiled; he was ready. “Yes,” he answered. We apply explainable AI, in particular, SHAP values, to analyze predictions. It demonstrates what characteristics have the greatest impact on the churn risk of a customer. The auditor moved his head in approval. Compliance does not merely imply the adherence to rules but rather it involves demonstration of accountability.

Discipline was necessary in terms of making compliance a part of the project. There were stage documents that were recorded by James, Clara and the data governance officer; the data sources, transformations, model validation and version control. Power BI reports were modified and compliance checks were added, which mask sensitive fields, including personal data. This was accompanied by a regulatory review gateway at the end of each sprint which was subsequently to become the standard practice at the company.

James thought of their advancement. An analytics was a professional instrument that was restricted to the data science team a year ago. It is at the heart of all the decisions today. Segmentation is an element of marketing that is used to customize retention campaigns. Finance uses risk models to obtain more correct credit scoring. Customer service also uses dashboards to put high-risk accounts on the priority list before being left. Analytics has become more of a strategic asset rather than a support aspect.

But most of all, this was the change in his leadership that shocked James. He did not view analytics as a technical discipline anymore but as a language, a connection between teams, systems, and goals. He was taught to decode information into uncomplicated narratives. In case a chart was down he said, What story does this tell? He wanted to know what it would mean to customers when a model predicted risk. Information that is transferred turns to empowering.

After a long conference that evening James sat alone in the office looking out over the Thames. The lights of the city glowed on the water, as points of a scattered mass that can only come together to make a figure at a distance. He opened the current churn dashboard. The retention increased, fraud cases decreased, and the cost of acquisition was lessened. Even more than figures he had a logical history in every measure. He grinned, and realized that this is what it takes to have a really data-driven management: technology, people, and purpose aligned.

Gradually, the lessons of FinSphere turned into a case study of the fintech. Smart analytics is not merely a reporting tool, but it leads to foresight. Adaptive thresholds were taken by the models of fraud, reducing false positives. Segmentation went beyond the demographic to behavioural clustering, which allowed customised experiences. The risk models were a combination of numbers and feelings that were combined with the customer sentiment. The combination of information and compassion turned out to be the latest standard of gold.

Technically the team continued their stack improvement. Python pipelines were used to do automated API ingestion. Stored procedures in SQL were used to faster queries on millions of rows. PowerBI dashboards were turned into powerful command centers with executives simulating changes on churn and compliance by adjusting limits of transactions or turning up alert sensitivity. The company did not sacrifice control and accountability in favor of innovation.

To James, the transformation reinstated one fundamental project-management reality that technology can only be effective when it fulfills human needs and moral expectations. In his last presentation to the board he showed three words: Data with purpose. He added that Fintech is based on trust. Trust requires transparency and transparency means analytics which predicts and explains. It is not about reducing churn, but about understanding customers in order to keep them.

Funds have been passed by the board to support more extensive analytics AI personalization and enhanced fraud detection. James also imposed one condition each model should be interpretable, each decision traceable. His data integrity was not a collection of numbers but values, he said.

The next step to take occurred a few months later, when a former customer returned and James received a note that a new feature was released by FinSphere called credit-insights. The note read I walked away as a false alarm had locked me out. I returned because I felt that the process was fair, and the service heard. James reread it. It was not just feedback, it was confirmation. All algorithms affect a person and all choices are responsibility.

In retrospect, James considered that the project was a human victory rather than a technology victory. Forecasting reduced turnover; care maintained clientele. Models were constructed using Python scripts; trust was constructed through collaboration. SQL combined data; common cause bonded teams. Numbers were displayed in Power BI, impact in leadership. Obledience did not suppress innovation, but put it in integrity.

The FinSphere narrative brought about the transformation of fintech- analysis, regulation, and customer-focus coming together. The modern fintech cannot afford to use speed as it is; they require accuracy, visibility, and vision. Patterns, meanings in behavior, risk, and relationships are also the objectives of analytics.

At the termination of the project, James prepared a final report. Some of the lessons that he condensed to help future managers are: analytics is a guiding tool, but not a destination. It takes one through the maze but requires application and reality to attain real outcomes.

The new challenge that James was soon confronted with was aligning analytics projects with regulatory compliance. Fintech Every model should have strict rules that include PSD2, GDPR, and local laws against money-laundering. Predictive analytics is effective, but it does not work alone. All the data fields and any model parameters should be traceable, explainable and auditable.

In one of the compliance reviews, an auditor had posed a query as follows: How do the decisions of the churn prediction model get made? James smiled. He was ready. "Yes," he replied. We interpret the model with explainable AI, i.e. SHAP values. They demonstrate what features will increase the churn risk of a customer. The auditor nodded. Compliance does not simply mean to adhere to the rules but to be accountable.

Discipline was added to the project lifecycle by including compliance. James worked with Clara and the data governance officer to record all the steps: sources of data, data transformations, data model validation, and versioning. The power BI reports were modified to include compliance checks by masking sensitive information like personally identifiable information. Regulatory review checkpoint was made to be done at the end of each sprint, which became a standard procedure.

James turned and peered over his shoulder. One year ago, analytics was an expert instrument of the data science team. It was now in the very heart of decision-making. Segmentation-based retention was applied in marketing. Risk models were applied with the use of finance in credit scoring. Dashboards were utilized to identify high-risk accounts at an early stage by customer service. Analytics became strategic and not a help.

The most important issue was how the project transformed James into a leader. He regarded analytics as not only technical effort but as a language: a connector between teams, systems and objectives. He got to know how to put discoveries into everyday language, numbers to narratives. When one of the charts declined he inquired, What is the tale of this? When one of the models raised a flag and notified that there was a risk, he would respond by asking what it means to the customer. Information was not also threatening but empowering.

One day, James was sitting solitary in the office with a view of the Thames after numerous meetings. On the water gleamed city lights like data points creating an image that could be observed only with distance. He went to his laptop and reviewed the churn dashboard. The retention increased, the fraud complaints decreased, and the cost of acquisition decreased. Even more so, each measure was a coherent story. He smiled. Authentic data based project management is where the technology, people and purpose are in tune.

Lessons at FinSphere were eventually a common fintech case study. Wise analytics is not only a reporting tool, but it is a foresight engine. The model of fraud was used to assume adaptive thresholds, which reduced false positives. Segmentation did not end at demographics to behavior so that it was possible to experience something personal. Sentiment analysis on customer chat was introduced to risk models, combining both numbers and feelings. Information and sympathy was the new gold standard.

The team continued to get better, technically. Python pipelines automated the daily data ingestion of API. SQL stored procedures increased the rate of queries on millions of records. Power BI dashboard became interactive command centers, at which executives experimented with strategic changes, such as the limits in transactions or the sensitivity of alerts, and viewed real-time forecasts of the churn and compliance risk. The company created a balance between accountability and innovation, agility and control.

To James, the change re-established an ancient fact: technology is only successful to fulfill the human needs and ethics. In his last board presentation, he displayed three words; Data With Purpose. He said, "Fintech runs on trust. Trust is based on clarity and clarity is based on the predictive and explanatory analytics. We do not simply want to reduce churn, we want to know our customers in such a way that they want to remain.

The board financed a larger analytics project - AI personalization and enhanced fraud detection. James made one condition, all models must be interpretable and all decisions traceable. Differing it not only by numbers, but by values, he said.

Several months later, when FinSphere was preparing another feature of credit insight, James received a message that showed the return of a former client. The message was, I went after a false alert lockout. I returned because the procedure was on the right side of things--and the service was attentive to hearing. James reread it. It was not feedback, it was confirmation. Every algorithm has an individual in mind and responsibility is attached to every decision.

In the retrospect of his venture, James considered the project as a human victory, rather than a technological victory. Forecasting analytics reduced turnover; sympathy retained clients. Models were made using python scripts; trust was built through collaboration. Data was combined using SQL queries; teams were brought together by a common purpose. Power BI represented figures; leadership emphasized influence. Conformity did not suppress innovation but pegged it on honesty.

The narrative of FinSphere reflected the overall trend of fintech: analytics, regulation, and customer-centered design meet. The contemporary companies cannot survive on speed but must rely on accuracy, openness and vision. Analytics goes beyond identification of patterns, it is finding meaning in behavior, risk, and relationships.

James wrote his final report when the project was closed. He identified important lessons to be used by future managers: Analytics is a guide, not a goal. It is able to make its way through complexity, but interpretation is required to realize real results.

CHAPTER 11

DATA GOVERNANCE AND ETHICS

•••■•••■•••

As Anita Khanna became a part of NovaCred a fast-growing fintech focusing on digital lending, it became clear that her utmost difficulty was trust, rather than faster algorithms or new features. The company had established an innovation brand where people could receive instant credit decisions with the help of AI. However, with the increase in the size of the dataset and complexity of the models, Anita felt that something crucial was lacking: organization, responsibility, and ethics surrounding the use of data.

The week that she first spent proved her right. During a product-strategy meeting, the data scientists were discussing the effectiveness of a new loan-approval modcl. Onc analyst boasted that the accuracy of the model had increased by 91 per cent since the addition of historical transaction data. All people applauded--except Anita. She moved forward and inquired, of whence the new data had come. Silence. The analyst responded by saying that we included a third-party data which monitors the customer spending trends. It is anonymized and we yet know not how it was gathered.

Anita saw a red flag. The only thing that counted was accuracy provided that data was ethically obtained and well governed. Her role as a new Director of Data Governance was to make sure that all data, models, and decisions were ethically and regulation-wise sound. To her, governing did not mean being bureaucratic, but rather acting with integrity.

She visualized an information ecosystem at NovaCred. The architecture was stunning but disorganized: banking APIs pushed and pulled transaction data, customer demographics existed in a CRM, behavioral data was available in the mobile app and model results were in disparate cloud repositories. All the departments had different datasets without uniform naming standards, quality measures, and accessibility. Users were able to query production data directly; analysts created dashboards without lineage documentation. It had ended in a weak environment that was prone to error--duplicate information, loss of privacy and uneven observations.

To correct this, Anita came up with a centralized data governance framework. She wanted to simply but radically change data to be reliable, compliant and ethical in its design. She informed the leadership that it was not about halting innovation, but rather facilitating it in a safe way. She said that without guardrails data-driven growth may lead itself over a cliff.

The initial action that she took was a background question: Who owns the data? The ownership was not well established- marketing owned customer data, operations owned transaction data and compliance owned risk datasets. The shared accountability was suggested by Anita. The accuracy of each dataset would have a Data Owner, Data Steward to maintain and a Governance Committee to oversee each dataset. She implemented these functions by bringing in a governance charter a constitution defining the ways data was gathered, stored, accessed and utilized.

She launched Collibra which is a widely used data governance tool. Collibra was converted into the data dictionary of NovaCred, where all data sets were registered. It provided users with the ability to trace lineage between the source API and end dashboard and displayed the data modifier and supported business processes. Such openness reduced bafflement that was bedeviling analytics discourse by half. Role-based access control and the masking or encrypted personally identifiable information were also applied by Collibra depending on the permission.

Anita used Collibra with Informatica Data Governance tools to automate quality monitoring. Rule-based profiling inspected incoming data sets on missing fields and format inconsistency as well as duplicates. Dashboards were used to identify anomalies in real time and automated alerts were used to alert stewards when some problems occurred. The absence of a credit-score value or an invalid national ID caused a ticket to be established which had to be resolved to allow the data to proceed downstream. These became the governance infrastructure backbone of NovaCred which gave visibility and accountability.

However, half the problem was taken care of by technical controls. The more serious issue was morals. The algorithms used by NovaCred looked at sensitive financial behavior, and thus minor biases would give out discriminatory results. Anita remembered a situation, in which another fintech had refused women at a disproportionate rate since the model had been trained on gender-biased historical information. She was aware that NovaCred was forced to avert such situations.

She brought the data -science team to discuss training datasets. Demographic breakdown, show me, she suggested. The team was hesitant with the fact that demographics were not used in predictions. Anita was aware of bias being indirect by having proxy variables; postal codes, levels of education spending category etc that were related to gender, ethnicity or income. In order to identify the latent trends, she initiated a fairness audit with the IBM AIF360 library. Even in the case of creditworthiness control, applicants in lower-income postal zones were found to have a 15 900% lower approval rate in audit. It was an unintentional outcome of biased data not a bad intention.

Anita has reported the findings in a composed manner to the leadership. And that is why the governance is important, she said. The best models, without ethical supervision, will turn into unfair gatekeepers. Her suggestions included the following correction: balance training data, add fairness constraints to model optimization, and create an Ethical Review Board to review the future algorithms. To ensure that ethical considerations are in line with the business objectives, the board would unite data science, compliance, and customer advocacy.

Privacy was a top concern. The GDPR and CCPA obliged NovaCred to secure the data of its customers and clarify the purpose of its usage. Anita used privacy-by-design to all projects. She has made anonymization and pseudonymization commonplace and hashes accounts and addresses using salted encryption and then feed them into models. She established a five-year retention policy: information over five years would be stored or removed unless it is legally necessary. Teamwork among various departments was required in these steps, which, however, was not a problem due to the clear communication of Anita. Rather than preaching about compliance, she demonstrated how ethical data management develops customer trust and provides NovaCred with competitive advantage in fintech.

In order to entrench governance within the company, Anita collaborated with project managers to include governance milestones in all the project charters. None of the projects could commence without a data impact assessment, which enumerated the sources of data, its intended use, and the security measures. Before the code started, the evaluation identified the privacy risks, ethics, and compliance requirements. There were also charters of data quality key performance indicators, such as completeness, accuracy, and timeliness, which needed to be monitored in addition to the normal project measures, including scope, cost, and schedule. Put simply, governance was measurable just like performance.

The strategy of Anita was based on a definite lifecycle. During initiation, governance requirements were specified and laid down. These rules were implemented automatically during the execution using such tools as Collibra and

Informatica. Power BI dashboards in the context of monitoring monitored compliance KPIs and highlighted datasets that had quality issues that remained unresolved or had outstanding audits. In the closing process, a governance review was carried out to ensure that there was no data handling that was unethical or illegal. This framework transformed a fixed policy to be a living, visible, measurable and actionable process.

The cultural change was the greatest beneficiary. Initially, the developers and analysts believed that governance entailed additional paperwork. Anita changed that view. She organized workshops in which teams would observe real-life examples of bad governance causing expensive errors, like a competitor that was fined 5M of the Euro because of misusing data, or a company that made 20 percent of a mistake in estimating loan risk. Her other demonstrations on how good governance enhanced teamwork were that data catalogs and lineage tracking enabled teams to understand which dataset to believe and where to get updates. The issue of governance was no longer a bottleneck but it became a compass.

In order to make the lessons practical, Anita presented a Data Ethics Simulation. The imaginary case studied by teams was a marketing campaign that used predictive analytics to offer loans to customers. The data encompassed history of spending and geography. The participants argued whether the practice complied with ethics and regulations. The debates were quite intense but created awareness. Others were in favor of innovation, and others of caution. Balanced, rather than absolute, ethical decisions were the result. Afterwards, Anita made a list of the most important lessons and created the first playbook of NovaCred of Ethical Analytics, a living code of responsible data practices.

In months hard data indicated improvement. Data quality scores rose 25 %. Audit findings fell sharply. Privacy complaints by customers were reduced to near zero. The governance program that NovaCred has developed was hailed by the regulators as a model in the industry. What was meant to be a correction turned out to be strategic credibility.

Anita stayed vigilant. Governance is not a task in itself but a journey. Ethical fronts that the emergence of AI opened were transparency, explainability, and accountability. She spearheaded the development of NovaCred Model Register, the standard place where all production machine-learning models are registered. The purpose of each model, model inputs, source of data, version history, and explainability reports are listed in each record. The register will allow the auditors to follow the logic and origin of every decision, which will comply with regulatory and ethical transparency expectations.

The Model Register links with NovaCred analytics stack through APIs. The metadata of a model (version number, performance metrics, and data dependencies) is automatically stored every time it is deployed. Python scripts are used to integrate model metadata with the governance catalog using Collibra REST API to provide end-to-end traceability. The data in the model is checked using Informatica workflows which ensure that it meets approved quality rules. Such smooth integration puts NovaCred in a place of unrestricted control and responsibility of AI lifecycle.

One night, at a later time, Anita monitored the compliance dashboard and received a desperate email in response to the first ones by a senior engineer. One of the partner companies sought to access anonymized customer data in co-research on credit-risk patterns. The set had transaction summaries and behavior profiles. The engineer requested to give it at once. Anita paused. It may not consider it dangerous to share anonymized data, but the risk of re-identification is still present. She commissioned a privacy risk evaluation prior to the transfer approval. The evaluation involved the metrics of k -anonymity and differential privacy to assess the ease with which people could be re-identified based on aggregate data. The risk was moderate in the report- some peculiar spending habits might be traced to individuals. More security measures were introduced such as random noise and category generalization, and then Anita was able to block the request.

The following week, the representative of the partner called her personally and demanded that the precautions were not necessary. Anita stayed firm. Not to be compliant, but our customers, I said. Trading privacy against convenience is impossible. Her position was also respected by executives and helped to portray the message of governance being all about principle and not procedure.

Unknown to the policies and platforms, Anita realized that governance is human in nature. It is based on awareness, empathy, and moral clarity. She also tutored young data analysts to think of the consequences of their work. When they constructed dashboards, she questioned, Who is this data telling? Who might it leave out?" As they cleaned data, she pointed them to the fact that they might be getting rid of real people with outliers. Through her teachings, a generation of professionals was created over time that viewed data as a duty, rather than a commodity.

At mid-year, the NovaCred analytics teams had completely settled in the governance structure. All the datasets were registered in Collibra, certified by Informatica and accepted by the Governance Committee. Each new project was initiated with an ethical impact statement a memo outlining how that project would fit into the company principle of fairness, transparency, and accountability. The company identity had been changed through the influence of Anita. What was previously a growth-seeking fintech company evolved to a data-responsible organization that is praised as being integrity-driven.

Anita proposed Ethical KPIs to measure the progress. These measures evaluated the morality performance of the organization alongside operational measures. Some of the KPIs were bias-reduction scores, DSAR response times, audit compliance percentages and a transparency index, which was used to assess how coherently the company reported the use of its data to its customers. These metrics were listed on the same dashboards with profitability and retention statistics, and it was revealed that ethics and performance were not independent, but rather supportive norms of success.

Technical maturity was also developed. The Collibra-powered automated tagging and metadata policies were now a part of the data lake of the company hosted in AWS. New data was fed into Informatica quality gates and Python programs verified the presence of schema, timeliness and integrity. Sensitive areas were encrypted with AES 256 and audit logs of all the access events were taken. NovaCred had developed an automated ecosystem upon itself where data flowed freely and control was not compromised.

When Anita gave a board presentation, she summarized her philosophy thus: governance is not about data being locked up. It is making it safe enough to share. She demonstrated the benefits of ethical practices of data in innovation. Under good governance, NovaCred may cooperate with regulating bodies, partners and research institutions without any fear of breaching of compliance. Openness was a competitive strength, which has been opened by the barrier previous lack of transparency had permitted.

The second project she undertook was Explainable AI. Regulators insisted on the explanation of automated decisions, in particular, the issue of loan approval and credit score as the predictive models became more complex. Anita and her team used SHAP and LIME to provide interpretability layers that enabled decision-makers to visualize which features had driven a model to output. In the event that a customer was rejected on credit, NovaCred now provided an easy-to-understand human explanation, e.g. inadequate history of repayment or high recent usage of credit, rather than esoteric arguments. This openness pleased the regulators and increased the trust of customers, as they were more willing to make the decisions that they could comprehend.

Transparency spread to communication. NovaCred revised its privacy policy and interface in the app to make information exposures more apparent. Instead of legal language, the customers did not see complicated text: We use your transaction history to offer you a better loan or You can choose not to share data. These minor design decisions made a significant impression. Customer survey revealed increased trust ratings in data handling by 30 per cent, which proved that ethics and the business results are connected.

Though successful, challenges still remained. The politics needed to be on high alert. There were new sources of data that were new risk. An error in the configuration during one system upgrade allowed a restricted number of anonymized logs to be revealed to a third-party tool. There were no delicate information that was compromised, and Anita handled it as a serious incidence. She introduced a post-mortem, found a rule of access-control that was not there, and put in place the automated scripts that checked such settings every day. Her motto was realistic but ideological: We do not conceal our errors. We get to know through them and ensure they do not recur again.

The incident strengthened the culture of accountability at NovaCred and demonstrated the worthiness of incorporating governance in project management. The DevOps group introduced a step in CI/CD pipeline, which is known as the governance validation. Above each code or configuration was an automated test that verified risks of exposed data, compliance tags and encryption policies. Such a combination made the ethical compliance a natural aspect of the development, rather than a bonus.

Anita had a bigger vision than NovaCred. She collaborated with other players in the industry to establish an ethical data governance fintech consortium. The organization wanted to establish unified biases reduction models, data disclosure, and responsibility of models. In one of the panel discussions, one of the journalists posed the question of why she was spending much on governance at a time when other competitors were focused on speed. She responded, recklessness is anarchy. Governance lends speed a conscience.

Several months later, NovaCred was mentioned in a global regulatory report as an example to follow in managing ethical data. The popularity increased the reputation of the company and brought in partnerships and investments. But Anita was more interested in internal change. She noted that the employees were now in the habit of doubting every decision and would ask whether it was in line with the company values before they embarked on a decision. The government was no longer her business and it was the duty of everybody.

Anita was late in the office on a rainy Friday night, and she was thinking about the journey. The Collibra dashboard was softly glowing in the light of the room and represented data lineage diagrams in the form of constellations of linked trust. This reminded her of the initial encounter several months back, when nobody was in a position to tell how the data was obtained. Now there was a story to each dataset, an owner to each story, and a responsible owner to each story. It was no longer a shadowy part of governance but NovaCred was the standard bearer of governance.

Her last action was to access the internal portal of the company and compose a message to be included in the Monday newsletter before closing her computer. The use of ethical data, she wrote, is not focused on avoiding errors, but making decisions that are respectful of people. A grain of someone life is attached to every transaction, to every model, to everything we establish, to all our insights. We should do that duty the dignity it deserves. she sent it, shut the laptop and walked away into the rain with a certain contentment.

Some weeks afterward, when NovaCred was ready to conduct the annual strategy meeting, the CEO invited Anita to introduce the meeting. She used her heart to address hundreds of her employees and partners. In the past, we counted improvements in the number of lines of code and gigabytes of data. Now we measure it in trust. Data governance does not hinder innovation, but rather forms the basis of innovation, which is sustainable. Ethics is not the price of doing business, but the motivation that customers will come to us.

Her words resonated deeply. By the time the applause had died away, Anita knew that the policies that she had promoted, privacy, fairness, transparency, had ceased to be a policy. They were now incorporated into the culture and conscience of the company. She made NovaCred measure its wealth not only in revenue but also in responsibility since this is a digital economy where data is the new currency.

Her work left a legacy even at NovaCred. Other fintech companies later adopted her model of governance with an aim of matching analytics with ethics. Her models, full of technical controls, compliance automation, and human-oriented guideline became a reference in conferences and whitepapers in the industry. She demonstrated a good governance does not suffocate innovation; on the contrary, it safeguards it.

Anita used to say that, water, like data, must have limits, in order to be purposive. Unrestrained it would burst and drown. It is able to foster growth with clearly defined channels governance policies, ethical oversight, technical controls. Information flow may be empowering rather than exploitative, informational rather than manipulative, and connecting rather than divisive.

Towards the close of this year of 2011 NovaCred had already established itself as a responsible analytics symbol. Regulators used its ethical AI practices as an example to other companies. Its transparency was believed in by the customers. Its integrity was something that the employees were proud of. And Anita, in the background, had heard that the government, serving its proper end, was not governance, but a kind of guarantee given to those whose statistics enabled all this to be so.

Her example showed that in the era of data, ethics is not a side add-on, but it is the design. Governance is not the foe of rapidity--it is the beat that maintains an advance in keeping with conscience. The systems she constructed, the tools she worked with and the culture she instilled all came down to a single living fact, that when data gets to be ruled with care and to be honored with respect it does not remain an asset. It turns into the embodiment of the most good intentions of humanity, organized, safe, and equitable.

CHAPTER 12

AGILE AND SCRUM IN DATA ANALYTICS PROJECTS

As the initial Carlos Mendoza entered the glass-walled meeting room, there was a sense of tension in the air. His team had been working weeks to provide insights to Trendline Stores which was the largest chain of clothes and accessories in the region. The client required a complete data-analytics product: demand forecast of the seasonal peaks, a tool of the inventory optimization, and the personalized recommendations to the online and to the brick and mortar stores. The project initially seemed exciting, however, it became a mess of delays, lack of purpose, and revisions. Analysts accused them of having vague requirements, engineers accused them of changing priorities, and the client accused them of slow progress. Carlos, being a certified Scrum Master and data-analytics manager, realized what was lacking the most - Agile discipline.

They had been defeated by the waterfall type management. Needs of trendline varied on a weekly basis as live sales figures, new promotions, and rival campaigns dictated the needs. The assumptions that supported the analytics team in one phase began to change by the time it completed the first phase. Carlos had observed this trend in other similar projects. In contrast to software development, data analytics is always exploratory; you can not determine all its requirements at the beginning since discoveries, experiments, and innovations are made along the way. This is why he decided to re-engineer the project using Agile and Scrum- a framework that is flexible.

The initial action he took was the initiation of a reset meeting. Inside the conference table, there were data engineers, business analysts, visualization specialists, and machine-learning developers. The walls used to be surrounded with whiteboards containing draft SQL queries, neglected process flows, and sticky notes with missed milestones. Carlos moved to the front and began to draw with his whiteboard a big circle and to write the only word therein: Value. He then included arrows out to the circle, which were labeled Data Engineering, Modeling, Visualization and Feedback. It is not only to create models, he started. We are committed to the provision of value, in a rapid, incremental, collaborative way. Since this day, we are going to use Scrum.

The party looked at each other with hesitation. Most of them had experience in Agile prior to this, but not many had encountered it used in analytics. Carlos preempted their suspicions. I understand that data projects are not the same, but Agile can be used here as well, given that we make the right adjustment to it.

He outlined clear roles. Carlos as Scrum Master would enable processes and eliminate roadblocks. A representative of each functional area would be nominated to be part of cross-functional Scrum Team: data engineering, analytics, visualization and business. Emma Clarke, the product owner of the client, who is a Trendline marketing executive with a keen sense of analysis, would place a premium on the Product Backlog. They would have Sprints every two weeks, brief and focused cycles that would result in tangible and reviewable deliverables.

The initial problem was to split analytics work into sprint-sized pieces. Several iterations may be made to build a forecasting model to give useful results. Carlos came up with iterative analytics increments. At the end of each sprint, something quantifiable would be provided: cleaned data, prototype dashboard, initial model, or an insight report. This was aimed at making progress visible and enhancing confidence by delivering continuously.

He established the Jira project foundation. Each sprint was initiated by a backlog-grooming, in which the team refined the user stories. Some of the epics that Carlos developed in Jira include Customer Segmentation Analytics, Inventory Optimization Model, and Demand Forecast Dashboard. Below each epic was a description of user stories in the end user perspective:

- "As a marketing analyst, I want to visualize customer segments based on purchase frequency and average basket size so that I can target promotions more effectively."
- "As an inventory manager, I want a predictive model that forecasts SKU-level demand by region so I can reduce overstock and stockouts."

Each story had clear acceptance criteria: "Segmentation must use at least three behavioral dimensions," or "Forecast accuracy must exceed 85% on validation data." This way, analytics tasks were not vague objectives but measurable deliverables.

Carlos also integrated **Confluence** with Jira to serve as the team's central documentation hub. Every model hypothesis, data assumption, and transformation logic was logged there. This transparency eliminated confusion between data engineers and analysts. When someone questioned why a particular dataset had been excluded from a model, they could trace the decision in Confluence documentation linked directly to the Jira ticket. For Carlos, this was crucial—documentation was the silent partner of agility. "Agile doesn't mean undocumented," he often reminded his team. "It means well-documented but never stagnant."

During the first sprint, the team focused on cleaning and consolidating sales and customer data from multiple sources. Data engineers built ETL pipelines in Python and SQL, ensuring all data from Trendline's POS systems, online sales, and loyalty app were unified into a single warehouse. Using Jira's Kanban view, Carlos could track progress in real-time: "To Do," "In Progress," "Review," and "Done."

Each morning, he facilitated 15-minute stand-ups where team members discussed what they completed yesterday, what they planned for today, and what blockers they faced.

"Yesterday I finished writing the SQL scripts for merging online and in-store data," said Priya, a data engineer, during one stand-up. "Today I'll validate timestamps and check for missing product IDs."

Carlos nodded. "Any blockers?"

"Yes," she said. "Some of the online transaction logs are missing region tags."

Carlos immediately took note. "Let's raise a Jira issue and assign it to the API integration team." Within hours, the blocker was addressed. That kind of responsiveness—something that rarely happened in traditional data projects—became their new normal.

By the second sprint, the team began developing the customer segmentation model. They used K-Means clustering in Python's Scikit-learn, applying it to the unified dataset. Each sprint ended with a **Sprint Review** meeting attended by the client. Instead of waiting months for final results, Emma could now see prototypes every two weeks. "These clusters look promising," she said, reviewing the first visualization dashboard in Power BI. "Can we add demographics to the segmentation?" The team added it to the Product Backlog for the next sprint.

This iterative loop of development and feedback transformed the project's dynamic. Instead of static deliverables handed over at the end, Trendline's stakeholders actively shaped the outcome. Carlos noticed that engagement increased and the client's satisfaction improved with every sprint. Agile had turned the analytics project into a collaborative learning process rather than a rigid execution plan.

One of the most powerful tools Carlos leveraged was **Jira's Sprint Burndown Chart**. It displayed how much work remained in each sprint, allowing him to detect early whether the team was overcommitted. In analytics, unexpected complexity often surfaced—data anomalies, unanticipated biases, or model instability. During Sprint 3, for example, the demand forecast model failed validation due to inconsistent seasonal trends. Instead of delaying the entire timeline, Carlos simply moved the incomplete story back to the backlog for refinement. Agile gave them flexibility without chaos.

Meanwhile, Confluence evolved into a living knowledge base. Every data dictionary, model parameter, and validation result was stored there, linked to the relevant sprint documentation. This practice not only facilitated collaboration but also ensured compliance. When auditors later requested a review of data lineage and analytical decisions, everything was traceable. Carlos realized that combining Agile with good documentation practices could satisfy both speed and governance—a lesson many analytics teams overlook.

From a technical perspective, the Agile approach also reshaped their architecture. Continuous integration pipelines were built to automate model retraining and data validation. Each sprint, the DevOps engineer deployed updates through Git and Jenkins, ensuring reproducibility. "Our sprints don't end with slides," Carlos often said. "They end with working code." That mantra resonated deeply across the team.

As the project matured, the team began tackling more complex analytics stories: sentiment analysis on customer reviews using Python's NLTK library, demand forecasting through Prophet models, and optimization algorithms for store replenishment. Each story was broken down into smaller, testable increments. For instance, one sprint focused solely on cleaning and tokenizing review text, while the next implemented the sentiment classifier. The incremental structure allowed stakeholders to see progress continuously rather than waiting for a grand reveal.

The **Agile feedback cycle** was especially valuable in refining models. After Sprint 5, the client's merchandising department tested the demand forecast dashboard and reported discrepancies between predicted and actual stockouts. During the next sprint planning session, Carlos facilitated a discussion on hypothesis testing. The analysts discovered that weather patterns, previously excluded, significantly influenced sales. They added historical weather data into the model and retrained it. By the next Sprint Review, accuracy had jumped from 82 to 90 percent. This improvement wasn't just technical—it demonstrated the power of iterative collaboration. Feedback wasn't an interruption; it was the fuel for refinement.

As project velocity improved, Carlos implemented **Sprint Retrospectives** to focus on process optimization. The team gathered at the end of each sprint to reflect on what went well, what didn't, and what could be improved. One recurring issue was sprint estimation. Analytics tasks often took longer than expected because of data unpredictability. To fix this, Carlos introduced "exploration spikes"—short, time-boxed research tasks used to assess data feasibility before committing to full stories. This technique allowed the team to balance flexibility with accountability. It became one of their most valuable Agile adaptations for analytics work.

From a project management standpoint, defining deliverables for analytics sprints required a new mindset. Instead of deliverables being final models or dashboards, they became *learning outcomes.* Carlos documented these as "Knowledge Deliverables" in Confluence. For example, "Validation shows the top five factors driving churn" or "Prototype model achieves baseline accuracy with limited features." These outputs, though not final products, still represented progress. This shift allowed executives to appreciate iterative discovery rather than demanding perfection upfront.

Jira and Confluence became the twin engines of visibility. Dashboards displayed sprint progress, backlog health, and burndown trends, while Confluence stored every assumption and experiment. When the client's CIO attended a Sprint Review session, she remarked, "This is the first analytics project I've seen where we always know what's happening. No black boxes." That comment, Carlos realized, was the ultimate validation of Agile success.

To further align with Agile principles, the team adopted **continuous stakeholder involvement.** Emma, the product owner, participated in daily stand-ups twice a week, providing immediate clarifications and reprioritizing backlog items as new business insights emerged. This level of collaboration kept the project aligned with real-world business shifts, especially during the retail holiday rush, when sales data changed dramatically. Agile allowed the analytics team to pivot quickly—retraining models, refreshing dashboards, and adjusting forecasts within days instead of months.

On the technical side, the team integrated **Jira Webhooks** with Power BI, automatically pulling sprint progress metrics into executive dashboards. These visual summaries gave stakeholders real-time visibility into velocity, sprint completion rates, and backlog trends. It demonstrated that Agile metrics could coexist with business analytics—data about the data process itself.

Carlos often reflected on how SCRUM had changed not only the team's workflow but their mindset. Collaboration replaced isolation. Iteration replaced perfectionism. Visibility replaced uncertainty. Most importantly, the relationship between data scientists and business stakeholders evolved from transactional to collaborative. Instead of being seen as service providers, the analytics team became strategic partners driving innovation.

By the project's midpoint, Trendline Stores began seeing measurable business results. Inventory turnover improved by 18 percent, seasonal demand forecasts became 30 percent more accurate, and targeted promotions based on customer segmentation boosted sales by 12 percent. These outcomes weren't the result of a single breakthrough but of cumulative progress across multiple sprints. Each increment contributed to a larger, adaptive solution.

Still, Agile in analytics wasn't without its complexities. One ongoing challenge was maintaining sprint cadence despite unpredictable data delays. When the external API providing competitor pricing data went down, the team's modeling tasks stalled. Carlos adapted by maintaining a "Technical Debt Backlog"—a list of tasks to improve code efficiency, documentation, and automation during downtime. This ensured no sprint was wasted and that the team maintained consistent rhythm.

Another complexity lay in sprint reviews. Unlike software features, analytical outputs could be subjective. A model might technically meet accuracy criteria but still fail to satisfy business expectations. To address this, Carlos introduced "insight validation sessions," where the client's domain experts tested analytical results against their intuition and operational knowledge. This step bridged the gap between algorithmic precision and human understanding—essential for analytics adoption.

Agile also helped foster a continuous improvement mindset in data engineering. Every retrospective generated technical optimizations: refactoring ETL scripts, improving data schema designs, or automating validation checks. The team established CI/CD pipelines for model deployment, integrating tools like GitHub Actions and Docker to package models reproducibly. Each model version corresponded to a Jira ticket, linking business requirements to technical artifacts. This level of traceability ensured that analytics outputs were not just experimental but enterprise-ready.

As the project neared completion, Carlos introduced one final Agile enhancement: **Sprint-Based Deliverable**

Definition Framework (SDDF) for analytics. The framework divided each sprint into four deliverable types—Data Deliverables (clean datasets, queries), Model Deliverables (prototype models, tuning reports), Insight Deliverables (analysis findings, visualizations), and Integration Deliverables (dashboards, APIs). Each category had specific acceptance criteria, ensuring consistency across sprints. This framework became a best practice adopted by DataVista's other projects later on.

The closing months of the Trendline project were a testament to Agile efficiency. The final model ensemble, combining time-series forecasts with regression adjustments, achieved 93 percent accuracy. Dashboards built in Power BI allowed store managers to view real-time sales forecasts, stock alerts, and regional insights. But what impressed the client most was the process itself. When the CEO attended the final Sprint Review, he said, "I've seen analytics projects fail despite good data. What made this one succeed was the rhythm—constant progress, constant alignment."

After the project's success, Carlos compiled a detailed case study for internal learning. He emphasized that Agile and SCRUM, when applied thoughtfully to analytics, required both technical rigor and adaptive leadership. Unlike software features, data insights evolved through exploration; therefore, flexibility had to coexist with structure. The combination of Jira for workflow, Confluence for knowledge management, and consistent stakeholder collaboration formed a triad that transformed analytics execution.

Carlos later trained other project managers in DataVista on how to implement Agile in data environments. He outlined several principles:

1. **Define analytical deliverables in measurable increments.** Even an exploratory task can have defined outputs—datasets cleaned, models benchmarked, insights discovered.
2. **Time-box exploration.** Limit data research to specific sprints to prevent endless experimentation.
3. **Integrate documentation.** Use Confluence or similar tools to record every decision, maintaining reproducibility and compliance.
4. **Engage stakeholders constantly.** Feedback loops refine models faster than isolated analysis ever could.
5. **Automate wherever possible.** CI/CD for analytics reduces technical debt and maintains delivery speed.
6. **Measure both process and outcomes.** Sprint metrics are as valuable as accuracy metrics.

As months passed, Carlos's success story became a model for other analytics teams across industries—healthcare, logistics, and finance—looking to implement Agile practices. His key insight remained consistent: Agile in data analytics isn't about fitting data science into SCRUM, but evolving SCRUM to respect the nature of data science.

Looking back at the Trendline project, Carlos recalled the early chaos of missed deadlines and disconnected efforts. What replaced it was a symphony of iteration—sprints, stand-ups, reviews, retrospectives—each piece harmonizing toward a shared purpose. The transformation wasn't just operational; it was cultural. Teams that once feared uncertainty now embraced it as part of discovery. Stakeholders who once demanded fixed outcomes now valued learning and adaptability.

One evening, as Carlos prepared the final sprint summary, he reviewed the Jira board filled with hundreds of completed tickets. Each represented a solved challenge, a tested model, or a refined insight. He realized that Agile wasn't merely a framework; it was a mindset—one that transformed analytics from a solitary craft into a collaborative engine of value.

When he delivered his final report to Trendline's executives, he summarized the entire project in one sentence: "We didn't just predict your sales—we built a process that keeps predicting, improving, and adapting." That, he knew, was the essence of Agile analytics: perpetual evolution.

As the meeting concluded and applause filled the room, Carlos smiled quietly. He had proven that even in the complex world of data and algorithms, agility was not just possible—it was essential. In a field driven by uncertainty and constant change, SCRUM had provided the one thing every analytics project needs most: clarity through collaboration, progress through iteration, and success through adaptability.

Table 1: Applying SCRUM Roles in Data Analytics

SCRUM Role	Data Analytics Equivalent	Responsibilities	Tools Commonly Used

Product Owner	Business Stakeholder / Client	Defines analytical objectives, prioritizes backlog, provides feedback	Jira, Confluence
Scrum Master	Data Analytics Project Manager	Facilitates sprint events, removes blockers, ensures adherence to Agile principles	Jira, Miro
Development Team	Data Engineers, Analysts, Data Scientists	Executes tasks: ETL, modeling, visualization, and testing	Python, SQL, Power BI, Git

Table 2: Sample Sprint Backlog for a Retail Analytics Project

Sprint	Deliverable	Description	Tools	Success Criteria
Sprint 1	Data Consolidation	Merge POS, CRM, and e-commerce data	SQL, Python	95% completeness across datasets
Sprint 2	Customer Segmentation Prototype	Identify initial customer clusters	Scikit-learn, Power BI	≥ 3 meaningful segments validated
Sprint 3	Demand Forecast Model	Predict product demand for 6 months	Prophet, Python	>85% accuracy on validation data
Sprint 4	Dashboard Integration	Build Power BI dashboard for demand trends	Power BI, DAX	Interactive and auto-refresh enabled
Sprint 5	Feedback & Optimization	Refine model based on sales feedback	Jupyter, Jira	Reduced forecast variance by 10%

Graph: Sprint Burndown Example (Analytics Project)

Work Remaining

```
|
|\
| \
|  \    *
|   \  *
|    \ *
|     *
|______*_________________________ Time
     Day 1   Day 7   Day 14
```

Legend:

- Line: Ideal progress

- Asterisks (*): Actual progress

This illustrates how sprint burndown charts track task completion in data analytics projects. If progress lags, the Scrum Master can identify blockers early—such as delayed data feeds or complex model tuning.

Table 3: Common Agile Metrics in Data Analytics Projects

Metric	Description	Purpose
Velocity	Number of story points completed per sprint	Measures team productivity and sprint predictability
Lead Time	Time between story creation and completion	Indicates efficiency of backlog management
Data Quality Score	Percentage of data passing validation checks	Tracks data readiness per sprint
Model Accuracy	Validation performance of models developed	Evaluates technical output quality
Stakeholder Satisfaction Index	Rating after sprint reviews	Monitors client engagement and trust

Table 4: Agile Tools Integration in Data Analytics

Tool	Purpose	Example Usage in Analytics
Jira	Sprint management and backlog tracking	Define epics for model development and dashboards
Confluence	Documentation and knowledge sharing	Record data assumptions, model decisions, sprint retrospectives
Power BI	Visualization of metrics and outcomes	Create sprint progress and data quality dashboards
Git / GitHub	Version control for code and models	Track model iterations and reproducibility
Jenkins / Airflow	Workflow automation and CI/CD	Automate model training and deployment per sprint

Table 5: Agile SCRUM Example Deliverables by Sprint

Sprint No.	Key Deliverable	Description	Stakeholder Value
Sprint 1	Unified Data Model	Combined CRM and transaction data into one schema	Enables holistic customer analysis
Sprint 2	Customer Segmentation Dashboard	Visualized clusters for personalized marketing	Improves targeting precision
Sprint 3	Forecast Algorithm	Model predicting demand per SKU	Reduces overstock and stockouts
Sprint 4	Automated Pipeline	Automated ETL for continuous updates	Reduces manual workload
Sprint 5	Model Deployment	Integrated forecast into retail system	Real-time business decision support

Table 6: Mapping SCRUM Ceremonies to Analytics Activities

SCRUM Event	Data Analytics Adaptation	Outcome
Sprint Planning	Define data stories, prioritize analytical goals	Aligned sprint objectives
Daily Stand-up	Review modeling progress and blockers	Real-time coordination
Sprint Review	Present dashboards and models to stakeholders	Business validation of insights

Sprint Retrospective	Evaluate process and model efficiency	Continuous improvement cycle

---

These tables and diagrams encapsulate how Agile and SCRUM bring structure, flexibility, and visibility to data analytics projects. Each visualization reinforces the concept that iterative delivery, collaboration, and transparent documentation transform data work into a measurable, value-driven process.

CHAPTER 13

BUILDING DASHBOARDS FOR PROJECT INSIGHTS

Maria Alvarez slightly changed the position of her chair, her eyes looking straight at the light that the monitor was giving out. It was almost 12 am, and the office of the consulting firm was already in its night mode with the only light coming from the screen, a quiet noise from the servers, and the rhythmic tapping of the keyboard were the only things that could be heard. In her mind, she was not just creating another dashboard. She was building a bridge-between the complex data and the clear understanding, the different teams with their common goal.

The logistics company that was supervising multiple regional rollouts was her next big project. Dozens of the tasks had been scattered across different teams, the milestones were getting delayed, and the costs were increasing slowly. The stakeholders were demanding one thing above all--visibility. They were not the ones to be interested in the raw data or even in the sheets filled with endless rows; what they actually wanted were the meaning, the context, and the story shown in one glance. And Maria, the senior project manager who was well known for her analytical acumen, made up her mind to produce exactly that with a Power BI dashboard.

She began with a simple yet profound question: "What story should this dashboard tell?" It was not about the colors or the charts but rather about the narrative flow. A good dashboard, Maria believed, was a conversation between data and decision-making. Each chart should address a stakeholder's question even before the question is asked. Her very first draft was not done on Power BI but was drawn on paper with boxes and arrows showing the relationships between Key Performance Indicators (KPIs): task completion rate, average time to closure, cost variance, and stakeholder satisfaction.

She had outlined the storyline the next day morning: Progress, Performance, Risks, and Value Delivered. These four panels would turn out to be the dashboard's backbone, thus, making the fragmented project metrics not only coherent but also actionable in the form of a story.

Prior to any construction, Maria accessed SQL Server Management Studio and started executing direct data queries. Data that is cleaned equates to insights that are credible. The system held numerous records of the tasks, along with their timestamps and completion tags.. She typed the command with care:

```sql
SELECT project_id,
    COUNT(task_id) AS tasks_completed,
    AVG(completion_time) AS avg_time
FROM project_tasks
WHERE status = 'completed'
GROUP BY project_id;
```

The query was very precise in the results that it returned — metrics related to the completion of each project were summarized in seconds. Maria then imported this data into Power BI. She also attached Excel files which contained the budget data and linked the live API feed from the company's project-tracking system. The dashboard transformed itself as it was listening to her commands.

Maria overlaid her visuals in Power BI. A stacked bar chart illustrated task completions per project phase. The line graph followed the average completion time over the last three sprints. A card visualization showed the on-time delivery percentage—updated daily. By using DAX expressions she was able to compute derived measures like "schedule efficiency" and "resource utilization index." Each figure was not just a number but a reflection of project health, which were the results of weeks of cross-functional effort.

One of her colleagues, Dinesh, came to see what she was up to in her cubicle that morning.

"You've been doing this all night?" he asked with a smile.

Maria gave a weak smile in return, "Yes—but see," she pointed to the screen. "This dashboard is our voice. The red spike that you can see last month? It's the time when we had to postpone the logistics rollout because the supplier confirmation was delayed. But when we compare it with the communication metrics, we understand the reason for the delay more accurately. It is not inefficiency—rather, it is dependency."

Dinesh moved his head nearer and was very much impressed. "So, instead of just reporting it, we are able to explain the dip now."

"That is right," she said. "It is the difference between a dashboard and a data dump."

The creation of efficient dashboards was not a matter of technical skill but empathy. Maria learned this point through her experience. Stakeholders saw data from their own perspective: executives would require trends and risk indicators, accountants would look for accuracy, and operations would need immediacy. While working, she had to weigh the pros and cons of the appearance and the correctness of the facts - use of colors to indicate urgency, drill-through option for more detail and tooltips for the non-technical viewers without giving them too much information.

Her design principles were simple:

- **Minimalism over clutter.** Too many visuals dilute meaning. Each chart had to justify its space.
- **Color with purpose.** Red for risk, green for growth, blue for stability.

- **Interactivity with restraint.** Filters were intuitive—time period, project region, team lead—allowing exploration without confusion.
- **Narrative continuity.** The dashboard should guide the user from overview to insight naturally.

After the layout was final, validation became Maria's main point of focus. She did a validation check where she compared data displayed in Power BI with that in Excel exports and also made sure they were in accordance with reports from the ERP system. The finance director, who had complained before, said that one of the main problems that caused the analytics tools to wrongly represent the totals was due to the usage of different fiscal calendars by different departments. Maria resolved this issue by aligning the hierarchies of the dates and time zones that came from different data sources, an operation which was minor but very significant in turning the confusion that might have resulted into trust.

By the end of the week, the working model was available for the stakeholder's comments. It was a boardroom full of the different department heads who together had a variety of perspectives. Instead of starting the presentation with a technical explanation as one would expect, Maria took a completely different approach and began with a story.

"This dashboard," she said, "is not simply about keeping tabs on it—it's about foreseeing it. Let me show you how."

Clicking the buttons one after another, she explained: "At the top-left corner, the current state of our KPIs is being closely monitored. Alongside, the graph here shows how fast the work was done—can you see how the steep rise of June corresponds to the effective use of resources after Sprint 3? That's because the reallocation of underutilized testers was done after the Sprint 3. There, cost variance is the only factor that causes the increase of the delayed procurement activities while when we add communication frequency on top of it, we get a clear cut explanation of the causes of the loss because proactive coordination was able to reduce it."

Executives leaning forward and paying keen attention to what was being said. The numbers they saw were now linked to phenomena and thus, the dashboard had made the executives go beyond just noticing the figures to gaining deep insights.

The moment of challenge then came.

"Maria, I don't really see how this is different from other financial reports. It looks just like another pretty visual to me. How do we know that the predictive capability of this dashboard is real?" the CFO asked.

Maria chuckled. "You're asking a very legitimate question. The dashboard we're talking about here is only one step away from our SQL backend. So every time you refresh it, it's a call for the newest data on completion and budget that is answered immediately. This is not a static report–it's a real-time one. Moreover, we have integrated Power BI's analytics pane, which uses exponential smoothing as a forecasting technique for projecting the future execution of tasks based on past ones, to do trend forecasting. Therefore, the line here"—her finger was at the line—"isn't just pointing out what it was, but also predicting what might be happening next month if the current trend continued."

The CFO's expression gradually turned more serious, and he seemed to be reflecting on what was said. "Therefore, this is where we see the first signs of impending trouble, isn't it?" he said slowly.

"That's right," she said. "It's like being able to anticipate danger before it happens."

During the weeks that followed, Maria took the initiative to develop the various dashboard platforms further. The use of dashboards by Tableau was made possible for the area-wise study where the visual elements of the story were of great importance whereas the Excel was kept as the layer for fast-access, in-depth, and detail-rich audit.

Each tool had its role:

- **Power BI** for live, interactive dashboards and KPI tracking.
- **Tableau** for executive storytelling and presentation-ready visuals.
- **Excel** for raw calculations, scenario modeling, and backup validation.

Maria created connectors so the three tools would all refer to the same source tables, thus avoiding version drift, which is a problem that occurs frequently in multi-tool environments. Her mixed ecosystem became a model of interoperability, where one tool had the function that the other tools lacked without duplicating the same functionalities.

In terms of project management, the dashboards were a tool that changed the way the team communicated. The weekly status meetings became from the boring shows of slides into the live explorations. Stakeholders treated the dashboards as their own and they filtered by team, region, or quarter, and asking the questions to which they already knew the answers. The project went from being reactive to proactive. Instead of saying, "What went wrong last month?" they started to ask, "What can we do differently next month?"

The cultural shift was enormous. Maria observed that even non-technical employees were using metrics more and more in their conversations. The operations manager would say, "Our task completion rate has risen to 87%," instead of "We're doing better." Numbers became a new language that the company spoke.

However, there were still some challenges. For example, when the data from one of the regional systems was delayed, the dashboards temporarily showed a false picture of progress. Stakeholders were very worried until Maria found the root of the problem—a failed nightly job that caused SQL synchronization to stop. She wrote down the event and set up an automated data validation step that would check for anomalies before publishing. The takeaway was that the dashboards should not be considered reliable unless the data pipelines are reliable. Automation, monitoring, and governance were not choices—they were the trust guards.

Additionally, she learned to control expectations. There were times when the stakeholders would ask for dozens of new KPIs because they wanted to keep track of everything from the team morale to the email response times. Maria had to tell them that too much data would make them lose focus. "Dashboards," she said in a meeting, "should be like a car's instrument panel—you only see what's essential to drive safely."

To embed this discipline, she introduced a Dashboard Governance Framework. It outlined:

1. **KPI Ownership:** Every metric had a defined owner responsible for its accuracy.
2. **Refresh Policy:** Data updates followed agreed intervals—daily for tasks, weekly for financials.
3. **Validation Logs:** Automated checks ensured completeness and consistency before each refresh.
4. **Version Control:** Each dashboard iteration was documented, ensuring reproducibility.

The outcome was not only of a high technical nature but of a well-developed organizational maturity as well. This is because data has become a common asset, rather than a fragmented artifact.

During the third quarter of the project, the measurable outcomes became visible. The time spent on reporting the project was reduced from five hours to thirty minutes per week. The decision-making cycles were 40% faster. Stakeholder satisfaction scores increased substantially and Maria's dashboard became the standard for other divisions. The regional VP even referred to it as "the most human dashboard" he had ever seen—not because of the visuals, but because of how obviously it conveyed the team's story."

Maria's final presentation and her thoughts summed up her belief:

"Dashboards are not about colors and graphs—they are about trust. Trust in data, trust in process, and trust in each other's accountability. A good dashboard not only shows the performance—it changes the behavior of the people."

Her influence went beyond the boundaries of her project. She took other managers under her wing and guided them in dashboard design. She was not only teaching them the technical tools but also the mindset—clarity, empathy, and continuous learning. To her, Power BI and Tableau were not the final goals but the means to an end which was organizational literacy. Every new project was, for her, a way to get better at helping teams visualize their success.

In closing the initiative, Maria drafted one final insight report for leadership:

Project Management Lessons Learned from Dashboard Implementation:

- Begin with questions, not visuals. Every chart must answer a real business need.
- Balance automation with oversight—human review ensures meaning, not just accuracy.
- Treat dashboards as evolving products; refine continuously based on feedback.
- Foster a data-driven culture where metrics spark conversation, not conflict.
- Remember: dashboards do not replace judgment—they enhance it.

When the final review concluded, the CEO looked at the main screen one last time. "This," he said, "is what insight looks like."

Maria smiled softly. The numbers on the screen flickered with life—tasks completed, time saved, risks mitigated—but what they truly represented was transformation. The organization had moved from reports to reflection, from reaction to foresight.

And Maria, once a project manager lost in spreadsheets, had become the architect of insight—a storyteller in data form, building dashboards not just to display progress, but to illuminate the path ahead.

CHAPTER 14

SCALING ANALYTICS ACROSS THE ORGANIZATION

The image of David Reynolds was on the upper level of the corporate headquarters in a glass wall, which was slowly reflected on the window, which overlooked the city. The construction had the beat of the modern efficiency silent, open-plan offices, glowing dashboards, and data that traversed networks connected on its network to all corners of the organization. The last time he had been appointed to the position of Director of Enterprise Analytics was only six months before, but his initial task was the largest project of his career: to expand analytics throughout the company.

It was not a small task. The company had expanded to become more of a global player than a local one with branches in marketing and finance as well as operations, human resources and customer interaction. They each possessed their systems, logic and culture. They had years of being separate islands of knowledge they had finance that tracked budgets, operations efficiency, marketing conversion funnels, and HR workforce analytics in silent spreadsheets. David now had to bring them into a single data-wise ecosystem.

The directive of the board initially appeared to be a misleading easiness: “We desire a common analytics strategy that would enable each of the departments to make informed choices based on data. David, however, was aware that scaling analytics was not just a technological upgrade, but it was a company change. It demanded new infrastructure, new habits and most importantly, new culture.

He recalled his week of the first week clearly. Introductory meetings were on his timetable. The heads of the departments received him kindly with enthusiasm, and under it he felt troubled. The CFO was securing financial systems, the marketing VP was rejecting dashboards as too inflexible amongst creative teams, and IT was already overloaded. David also understood that opposition would not be based on lack of knowledge but rather on incompatibility of incentives and the fear of losing control.

Patience was his initial principle. He said to himself change must be won by trust, not by policy.

He started with mapping the landscape. His team received data and pain points in every department. Finance lamented on getting duplicate reports and differences in numbers between ERP exports and Power BI dashboards. According to marketing, said analytics came late, by the time campaign outcomes were received, the customer behavior was changed. Operation desired predictive maintenance but did not have data integration between the sensors and core systems. HR desired knowing how the turnover occurred but did not have interdepartmental data to compare job satisfaction with working load.

These problems depicted a trend. It was not the question of tools, but rather of fragmentation. Various systems, unlinked processes and a culture where data was viewed as departmental property and not a shared resource.

To address it, David constructed three things, including infrastructure, training, and culture. Technology provided the muscles, training provided the brains and culture, the hardest and most important thing of all was made the heart.

He began with infrastructure since analytics trust commences with reliability. Data in the past existed on different departmental servers which were also localized but not department wide. David suggested a hybrid cloud warehouse on Snowflake, to be scaled with controlled access, and AWS Redshift as the processing analytics of large volumes. Power BI would be the most important visualisation tool, associated with it through secure connectors.

The size initially fizzled the IT department. The migration would entail terabytes of structured and semi structural data and cross-regional synchronization. However, David treated it as a project manager, subdividing the massive goal into stages, each having quantifiable milestones. Phase one: report finance and HR data on Snowflake. Phase 2: add marketing and operations pipelines to Redshift to do high-achievement analytics. Phase three: consolidate access using power BI workspaces with balanced measures of visibility and control governance policies.

All the phases were framed in business terms, rather than in technical terms. The value to the executives was more speed in insight, reduced reporting conflicts, and cross-functional visibility. David won early supporters by converting the results of analytics into financial terms, e.g. cut the number of monthly reporting periods by 40 percent or increased the accuracy of forecasts by 15 percent.

The initial trial of the new infrastructure was in the quarterly forecasting cycle. Historically, finance and sales reconciled figures within a period of two weeks. On Snowflake, the pilot team of David reduced the time to two days. Revenue projections, supply -chain metrics, and market data were automatically aggregated through Redshift connectors. Analytics dashboards provided by Power BI provided a single forecast view that could be filtered by region or product line in real-time by executives. It was the first time when all the people in the leadership meeting were looking at the same numbers- there was no discussion of whose spreadsheet was correct.

The first person to accept the breakthrough was the CFO. I have the same figures operations has, I can see, clicking through the interactive view, she said. “This changes everything. No more shadow versions.”

David smiled quietly. It was not just technology that had worked out but it was conformity. The tool had created a trust where there was confusion.

Scaling insight could not be done solely by technology. The second bottleneck was capability after the success of the pilot. People who are effective are the tools. He observed that analysts and data engineers were able to prosper in the new ecosystem, but several mid-level managers failed. Others were afraid to open the dashboards in the fear of breaking it. Others read into pictures and came up with erroneous conclusions in trend lines.

It was at that point that David understood that the next frontier was training, but not some general software tutorials, but role-based analytics literacy. He collaborated with the HR and Learning and Development to establish an all-inclusive program named Data for Decisions. All workers, starting with the project coordinator and up to the senior vice president, were plotted into one of three levels of literacy, which include data consumer, data practitioner, and data strategist.

Training was offered to data consumers on how to read dashboards, how to understand metrics and how to pose the correct questions. To practitioners, the program was practical and applied PowerBI and simple SQL to access Snowflake datasets with a minimal IT assistance. The strategies of the leaders of the departments and senior leadership were taught how to integrate analytics into decision-making and governance frameworks.

Some of the initial workshops were personally conducted by David and abstract examples were substituted with actual company data. During a memorable session, he displayed a Power BI dashboard that displayed real-time customer-service response rates and inquired: What is the story behind this?

At first, the room was silent. One of the managers blinking back and forth said, “The response times seem to be getting better. Another retorted, Why did they spike last month? David smiled. “Exactly. You are now thinking like an analyst.

He also showed how to drill down, filter by region and read seasonal patterns. At the conclusion, even the most non-technical respondents would be playing with visual filters and cross-referencing KPIs. It was not about training but empowerment.

Analytics literacy was soon to be a common language. Project managers started to give the updates on the Power BI itself rather than on the static slides. Marketing was also using Redshift queries to identify trends of customer-retention per campaign. Using the data provided by the Snowflake dashboards, HR preempted workload-related attrition by analyzing engagement surveys.

Culture began to shift.

Scaling analytics did not only entail the development of new skills but also the development of a collaborative attitude. To promote that, David started the Analytics Guild the cross-departmental group, which held monthly meetings to exchange knowledge and present dashboards and discuss difficulties. Participation was voluntary and it increased rapidly. Finance analysts were discussing query optimization with operations heads, marketing experts were talking about the visualization methods that made the executive reports easier to understand. The guild over time emerged to be a grassroot source of innovation.

A collaboration between marketing and HR produced one of the initial success stories. Combining customer-feedback sentiment and employee-satisfaction data, they found that areas that were more engaged produced consistently more customer satisfaction ratings. This was not a coincidence but rather a measurable relationship which led to the focused engagement programs which made it a point of interest during the leadership summit.

In the case of David, this was the point when he realized that the transformation was actually becoming established. The analytics was no longer departmental but organizational intelligence.

However, there were new complications with scaling. The more users were accessing shared data the more governance and security concerns were brought up. One morning he got a notification that an unauthorized Power report, with old figures, was published. It was unintentional yet misleading executives reading KPIs. David then held an emergency meeting with his data governance council which he had previously established.

Three of the corrective measures he suggested are role-based access controls in Snowflake, centralized audit logs in power-BI and enforcing data-validation processes before a dashboard is shared. The plan was unanimously endorsed by the council, who consisted of the representatives of each department. The controls were established within a week making a possible crisis a reinforcement of trust and discipline.

On the strategic level, David knew that communication is important. Scaling was not about the implementation of technology, but a perpetuation of faith. Milestones were communicated throughout the whole company and every success story was made public. When the processes of finance cut reconciliation or marketing hits predictive targeting accuracy, the stories were aired throughout the company to demonstrate that analytics was a source of pride and not a burden.

As a quarterly, some tangible effects had been experienced. The operational efficiency increased in the double digits; the time taken to make decisions also reduced; and the dependency between departments became transparent, and therefore, the leaders could predict the conflict and not react to it.

David further warned that analytics will be overwhelming when used without balance as with any other potent tool. During one of the leadership meetings, an executive who has heavily depended on a specific predictive model proposed radical savings in areas that are not performing well. David pointed out, models direct us, they do not replace us. Strategy should not be determined by analytics, but rather supported by it. The caution was taken heed to.

The second obstacle was the international level. Latency and compliance became very important with regional offices in three continents. With AWS Redshift Spectrum, the team of David optimized queries in distributed warehouses without violating local data protection regulations. The role-based controls at Snowflake have ensured that European teams were within the bounds of the GDPR, and the divisions in the U.S. had the freedom to perform. The architecture was made a prototype of federated governance, centralized theoretically and decentralized practically.

Culture was the living variable even though infrastructure had grown up. One of the operations managers posed the following question at an event at a regional town hall: "David, how do we internalize analytics in our day-to-day practice, not quarterly meetings? David hesitated, and responded, "Analytics is an element of everyday work when it is motivated by curiosity and not by compulsion. Question everything by opening a dashboard since you want to know, by asking it questions and by letting it refute your assumptions. The motto of the transformation was made to be curiosity over compliance.

Months afterwards, when the program was to be fully deployed, David checked progress reports. The adoption of analytics was 92 percent interdepartmental. More than 700 employees were literately certified. Mean speed of dashboard increased by 60%. Turnaround time had also been reduced by half; that is, the time taken to request data and take an action. Numbers he recalled, were part of the story. It was the real turnaround of conversations being the discussions that took the lead of meetings. Arguments that used to be full of accusations turned to facts and trends overcame conjecture.

The question that the CEO raised one afternoon in the middle of an executive strategy meeting would have been viewed as a hesitation in the past: where are we going to expand next regionally?

David, without losing a second, brought up a consolidated Power BI dashboard which was utilizing data from

Snowflake and Redshift. He then went on to filter the data in terms of profitability, customer growth, and logistics efficiency. Not long after, a heat map showed the vibrant clusters that were performing well in Southeast Asia.

"Our growth is not just a flash in the pan of these markets but a steady trend and they are at the same time showing a high level of operational resilience," he pointed out. "The logistics data we have is perfectly matching with the trends in customer acquisition. We are not only told by the figures where we are succeeding but also the reasons for it."

The CEO agreed with the statement by nodding. "That is the difference," he confirmed. "We are not guessing anymore."

David was still looking at the dashboards long after the meeting had ended. It was not a sprint to scale analytics but rather a marathon that required persistence and the power to persuade. There were times when he felt frustrated and even thought that he had failed. It was said that the early versions had broken. The low turnout for training sessions was spoken of, and some teams going back to their old ways before finally embracing the new ones. However, through all these trials and tribulations, David came to the realization that the real thing to change in the company through analytics was not to convert the skeptics but to get more believers.

He viewed the journey in terms of three aspects: technology, trust, and transformation. Technology had provided the base; trust had been the pillar; transformation had made it valuable.

At that time, while walking past the conference rooms with glass walls, he saw the lights of what the future held success to be. People working together over the live dashboards. Managers going through the performance metrics side by side, rather than arguing over them. A marketing analyst breaking down Redshift query outputs to a finance controller in a very easy way. The silos were breaking down. The culture was changing.

At his place, he looked at one last report—an analytics maturity assessment across the company. The organization had made a leap towards what the consultants had initially termed “analytics-aware” to “analytics-driven.” Almost every vital decision was now backed by at least one data source from the enterprise warehouse. The transformation was over, although David was aware that in reality, it would never be over. Scaling analytics was not a location but a continuous journey of adaptation, improvement, and learning.

Shortly before going to bed, he put a short reflection into the company’s internal knowledge base, addressed to all teams:

"Analytics only succeeds when it ceases to be a department and becomes a habit. It is not the prerogative of data scientists or IT alone, but that of every professional who seeks clarity in complexity. The real accomplishment is not in the construction of dashboards or pipelines but in the creation of a culture that prioritizes evidence over assumption, collaboration over isolation, and insight over intuition. When data is the language of all, the organization becomes truly intelligent."

He reclined his chair and pondered over the words. The city lights were twinkling resembling nodes on a network—each one shining on its own, but connected with invisible threads.

That, he believed, was the ideal metaphor for what he had accomplished.

It was not about linking machines to scale analytics, but about connecting minds.

And if curiosity were to be the driving force behind those minds, then the organization would never cease to learn.

CHAPTER 15

PROJECT INITIALIZATION: FROM VISION TO EXECUTION

Elena Martinez was widely recognized as a visionary thinker in her company–a strategist whose ideas could make the figures tell stories and turn abstract objectives into real expansion. However, on that warm Monday morning, when light was coming in through the huge windows of her office located in the city center, she was confronted with a problem that was beyond even her brilliant intellect, i.e. how to convert her daring business idea into a concrete, data-guided project plan.

The company where she worked was a mid-sized retail firm planning the launch of a customer analytics platform that would be able to predict buying trends and personalize promotions instantly. The concept had been raised during the executive brainstorming session, and the only thing everyone agreed upon was that the future belongs to those who have better data. Nevertheless, Elena, upon looking at her notes, thought that having an idea was just the easiest part. The real task was to create an executable, measurable, and sustainable project where leadership starts to show.

The project carried high expectations and even higher risks. The CEO wanted to see the first prototype in four months. Finance was looking for a measurable ROI within a year. Marketing wanted to use their CRM system fully, while IT was cautioning that old data structures would make the process slower. Each stakeholder was asking for something different, and Elena had to dig this chaotic tempest of aspirations out and bring her order.

Elena decided to organize her thoughts by writing a plan. She turned on her laptop, started Microsoft Project, and began with the only sensible point—project initiation.

Project initiation, she thought, was not about immediately going into the execution. It was about understanding—bringing vision down to framework, resolving ambiguity with a roadmap. It was the connection between "what we want to achieve" and "how we will do it." In her view, the majority of projects that had failed were not due to execution mishaps, but rather because of the collapse of the planning phase where the failure to challenge assumptions, acknowledge risks, and build timelines based on evidence instead of being overly optimistic took place.

Her first task was defining **scope**. She called it "drawing the boundaries of the dream." She created a new document in

Monday.com and titled it "Customer Analytics Platform – Phase 1: Discovery and Build." Under the "Objectives" column, she listed the three measurable goals:

1. Develop a predictive analytics dashboard for customer behavior.
2. Integrate the platform with the existing CRM and ERP systems.
3. Deliver an interactive Power BI report for executive decision-making.

However, scope definition was more than just writing the deliverables. It was about figuring out what was not included as well. Therefore, in another column she wrote the exclusions: "No mobile app in this phase," "No AI-driven chat features," "Limited to North American customer data." This precision would be her shield when stakeholders would request additions to the project later on.

After that, the resources to be used were defined. Elena was of the opinion that project resources were not only people but also tools, data, time, and focus. She launched Excel and started her resource matrix. One axis contained roles—project manager, data analyst, data engineer, UX designer, QA tester, and business stakeholder.

The other axis contained estimated hours per week, allocation percentages, and dependencies. While she was populating the sheet, a pattern that was coming to light caught her eye. The analytics team was heavily loaded with work, while the design team had some free capacity. This disparity could cause bottlenecks halfway through the project.

She changed the allocations, turning one part-time data scientist into a full-time role for the first three sprints. The exercise, though not very exciting, was essential. Projects do not fail because of bad ideas - they fail due to poor capacity planning. When the resource matrix was done, she went to MS Project again and started putting together her Work Breakdown Structure (WBS)-the core of every project plan.

Her screen filled with branches like a living tree:

- Project Initiation
    - Define scope and objectives
    - Identify stakeholders
    - Develop project charter
- Data Infrastructure
    - Extract legacy CRM data
    - Clean and validate datasets
    - Build data warehouse in Azure
- Dashboard Development
    - Design wireframes
    - Develop Power BI reports
    - Conduct user acceptance testing
- Deployment & Review
    - Pilot with marketing team
    - Gather feedback
    - Finalize documentation

Every item was quantifiable, and each deadline was obvious. The WBS changed the abstract idea to real work. Besides that, it also functioned as a psychological anchor—when people saw that the complexity was organized, their fear was replaced with focus.

The Gantt chart was her next weapon. She was quite happy while connecting and dragging tasks in MS Project, and watching the dependencies forming lines between milestones. The horizontal bars were going far weeks, not only showing what would happen but also when. This timeline was far from being just a schedule—it was a living promise. It was showing the executives to whom she was reporting that the vision had turned into the actual work.

While she was plotting each dependency Elena was also doing what she termed "schedule empathy". She was not imposing the dates illogically; rather, she was considering how each task affected the other and, even more, how a delay in one place would cause a ripple effect on the whole timeline. She organized weekly meetings between the analytics and IT teams to make sure there would be no integration delays, thus saving the team from the trouble of redoing the work.

By the end of the day, the Gantt chart was ready. Each deliverable had owners, deadlines, and cushions for unexpected challenges. Nevertheless, no plan would be complete if it did not acknowledge the unknown. Therefore, risk planning was the next step.

Elena created another sheet and named it Risk Register. She put in one column potential risks, in the next one their likelihood, and in the third one their impact. She filled in rows with a mix of foresight and caution:

- **Risk:** Data inconsistency between CRM and ERP systems.

  Likelihood: High

  Impact: Critical

  Mitigation: Conduct data validation sprints before integration.

- **Risk:** Resource turnover mid-project.

  Likelihood: Medium

  Impact: High

  Mitigation: Cross-train team members on overlapping tasks.

- **Risk:** Delayed stakeholder feedback during testing.

  Likelihood: High

  Impact: Medium

  Mitigation: Schedule fixed feedback windows and escalation protocols.

A risk entry was not just a line on a paper: it was a leadership action. Risk planning did not involve predicting failure, but being respectful of complexity.

She completed this as her phone gave her a calendar notification of an executive kickoff meeting the following morning. She looked through her slides one more time. They were straightforward and had no jargon or polished graphics.

They narrated a story instead, on how the vision was transformed into execution, with structure, data and clarity.

On the following day, the waiting-room of the conference room was filled with anticipation. The heads of departments were sitting around the table with their laptops and coffee cups boiling. The CEO leaned forward. Well, how do we make this idea happen, Elena, he said. She plugged in her laptop into the projector and started.

All projects begin as ideas but only idea succeed when they are put in the context of structure. This is how we achieve this vision in a measurable result.

She used the WBS to walk them through and how every objective is broken down to smaller, responsible tasks. She thereupon drew out the Gantt chart. This is a timeline based on reality rather than optimism. We have developed dependencies, review cycles and risk buffers. It is not only a schedule it is a promise of predictability.

The first question was by the CFO. So how do we make sure that this is fitting our analytics strategy?

Elena smiled. "That's precisely the point. Each milestone is interlinked with a quantifiable analytics objective data preparedness, predictability, and clarity of a visualization. It is not the technology, but visitor. The achievement is to provide knowledge, and not the software.

The room quieted. The CEO nodded. "I like that. Keep going."

She moved to her risk matrix. There is a mitigation plan and mitigation owner of each of the risks here. Uncertainty is something that we cannot control, but we can plan it.

The IT director leaned in. What is the dependency of our systems with the marketing API?

Already mapped, I said, and clicked to a dependency view in MS Project. We have aligned the milestones on integration with your deployment schedule. Three weeks prior to the API being live, the data warehouse team begins to test. No blind spots."

At the final part of the meeting, doubt was transformed into belief. Her plan was unanimously passed by its executives. The CEO ended the session by stating that, this is how vision becomes execution, one planned plan at a time.

During the further weeks Elena project was the prototype of the way the initiatives ought to start. Her WBS was clear and it helped in team discussions. The Gantt chart held everyone on track with regards to timeframes and the risk register avoided crises prior to their occurrence.

She used Monday.com to update the team every Monday morning and see the progress of tasks visually on the dashboard. Progress bars were also in place color-coded: green on track, yellow at risk, and red delayed. The accountability established by the transparency was non-confrontational.

The risk plan became activated when timeline was threatened by a delay during data migration. The cross-trained engineer whom she had used before intervened without trouble and the time lag was swapped in the buffer that was built in. This was when the planning worked.

However, the strongest one was probably the moment of the mid-project review. When the team was meeting to evaluate the progress, Elena displayed the Power BI dashboard with live metrics fetched in the project logs. It presented earned value, resource utilization and schedule performance index all dynamically computed.

This is not project management, said she. This is analytics presiding over execution.

The project was also completed a week earlier and on budget. The new analytics platform was launched with little problems and soon started to create the insights that assisted the marketing boost the rates of conversion by 18 percent within the first quarter. The CEO publicly complimented the undertaking as being the textbook example of data-driven implementation.

The actual winning point to Elena was not on-time delivery, but the practice of transforming grayness into black and white. She used to think that project initiation was laying a foundation. The other parts of the building would only be able to hold their own weight when the initial layer was very accurate, was quantitative and data based.

Several months later, she was requested to mentor a team of younger project managers. They desired to understand her way of successful project launches. She grinned, and said to them what life had taught her:--You start every fine enterprise twice, once in plan, and once in reality. One is inspiration, the other is execution. Tools are not sufficient to bridge them. It is a process of patience, accuracy, and boldness to establish the vision of success before the work has started.

Then she stopped and added, a vision without a plan is a dream. Yet a strategy based on information, scope, plan--that is leadership.

The new managers sat there in silence, taking in whatever she was saying, as she left the room. Elena was aware that they, too, would one day be in the same situation that she had been standing by the window between the vision and the reality, between the idea and the deed. And when that day would come they would recall that all successful projects do not start in motion, but in clarity.

To Elena that was the long lesson of her journey that project start-up is not the prelude to project execution--it is the highest, the tightest form of project execution.

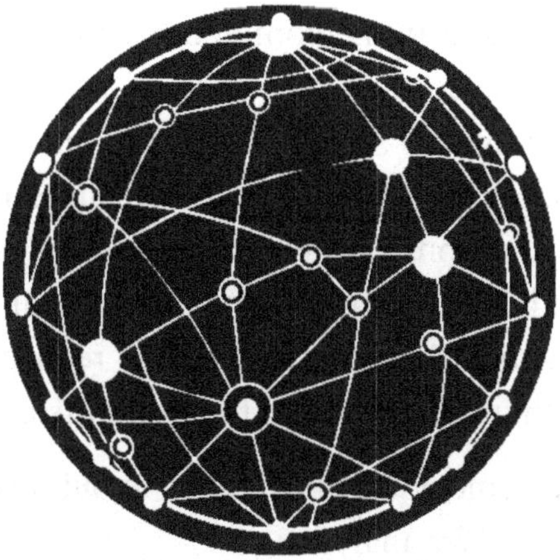

CHAPTER 16

THE FUTURE OF DATA ANALYTICS IN PROJECT MANAGEMENT

John Matthews sat back in his office chair and looked out over the skyline which was shining in the late-afternoon sun. His office was silent; the chatter whose song was habitually heard, was in its place by the pawing of city traffic. His desk was lit by two screens, one with a live project dashboard, and the other one with predictive insights, delivered in real time by an AI-based analytics engine. Almost poetically he imagined the extent to which things had gone.

The project management tools that John used at the start of his career in the field twenty years ago were primordial, consisting of Excel spreadsheets, blank Gantt charts, and printed status reports that would have become outdated before they made it to the conference table. The interaction was based on never-ending emails and late-night calls. The progress tracking was slow and was not updated frequently and could be weeks away. There was more intuition than logic in the decisions. He was now seeing the technology, analytics and human insight concur in real time on his PowerBI dashboard, and it made him realize that he was seeing something never before thought possible.

Project management was no longer about analytics, but it was now defined by analytics.

This was not theoretical change to John. He had grown through the evolution. He had faltered over the process of changing the conventional control to the one based on data and made it his best asset.

He could recall his initial experience with predictive analytics clearly. Almost a decade ago, his business started to incorporate initial machine-learning algorithms as a part of project surveillance. The models had flaws however they were radical: vision. John was able to anticipate schedule delays rather than responding to them. The algorithms examined the trends in task completion, use of resources and patterns of communication among teams. They taught that when internal email traffic increased on Thursdays, there was likelihood of slippage in the milestones the next week.

Initially, it was scorned by a number of colleagues. Projects are not understood by a computer, a top-level manager sneered. Yet something deeper John perceived. Analytics was not taking human judgment over, but enhancing it. It appeared that the fog of uncertainty that had necessarily hovered over projects was being cleared away.

In 2030, the change had taken place. Analytics were now the blood of the project management circulating insights that kept the decision-making flowing throughout the organization. AI did not simply analyze information, but it organized it. Live performance measurements of factories, logistic and construction sites were pushed into dashboards using IoT-based devices. The project planning process was living and breathing because machine-learning models constantly re-calibrated predictions using new data.

John looked at the bottom right of his screen where a blinking notification was showing: AI Risk Monitor: Schedule variance in Plant Expansion Project predicted at 6.4. He opened it and read the information. The system had identified micro-change in production throughput with the help of the IoT sensors, cross-linked, and decided that one of the milestones could be missed by four days. It even provided remedial measures: redistribution of labor, speed up purchase, or a change of the buffer in the downstream schedule.

He smiled. He would get to know this ten years later after the delay, he muttered.

This was the era of real-time analytics, which was a long way away back in his early days with the reports which were not dynamic. Management of projects was no longer done on a snapshot basis; it was done on a stream basis. All the decisions including resource allocation and procurement were based on real-time data. Artificial intelligence was the context, IoT was the immediacy, and the cloud-based platforms were the scale.

Yet despite all this technology John was sure of the human aspect that could not be substituted. He had witnessed the collapse of organizations that were using the best analytics tools. The omitted element was the same one, culture. The culture of data-driven did not appear due to software licensing or dashboard, but it was the mindset. It entailed training teams to pose the correct questions, rely on evidence and not hierarchy, and look at analytics as a team effort as opposed to a form of control.

He recalled an experience at the beginning of the analytics transformation of his current company. The AI system raised an alarm over supplier delays but it was disregarded by the procurement manager who insisted that this information was inaccurate. Three weeks later when the shipment was late, John convened a meeting, not to rebuke, but to instruct. The facts were not false, he replied to them. "We just didn't trust it. Analytics does not mean substituting your judgment- it enlightens it. It is a discussion between experience and evidence.

That discussion was a turning-point. The company gradually incorporated analytics in their DNA. Dashboards, rather than reports, were used in meetings. Data scientists and project managers sat together when discussing strategies. Predictive dashboards were used even by the executive board when making decisions. The organization gained self-consciousness, a company that gauged its performance and improved it on a constant basis.

The newest development is something that interested him intensely: the combination of blockchain, ERP, and fintech systems to achieve sophisticated analytics. These technologies erased the distinction between the project management and the organizational intelligence.

Trust and traceability is one of the most ancient problems that were answered by blockchain in the context of project management. Vendor payments were now controlled by smart contracts, which discharged money after milestones were confirmed by data on the IoT sensors. This eradicated conflicts and minimized administration overheads. All the actions were verifiable and fixed.

ERP systems evolved too. They were not merely containers of transactions anymore; they turned into data engines that aligned finance, procurement, HR and operations into one analytical ecosystem. ERP data could now be used to continuously feed predictive models because project cost overruns could now be forecasted several weeks beforehand.

Budgeting became transformed by Fintech integration. The algorithms used machine-learning to study historical costs, and generated the optimal cash flow optimized between projects. Finance and project management were no longer distinct areas, they were connected to each other in real-time analytics, and all dollars were not only tracked but smartly used.

John was reviewing the changes that had taken place and viewed the modern project manager as a part strategist, part data scientist and part change agent. The instruments were different and the expectations, too. Running schedules and budgets was no longer a sufficient task, but it was a necessity to perform some analysis of data and become an innovator and change faster than ever.

He recalls the days when he used to go and update Excel dashboards manually and question their validity. His Power BI platform was now synchronized with Snowflake, Redshift, and IoT networks. Data pipelines were automated and were continuously verified on an ongoing basis by AI-powered integrity tests. His job was not to construct reports, but to pose even more profound questions: What does this trend mean? How can we respond faster? What is the opportunity behind this anomaly?

At least, that, he said to himself, was the new art of project management, which was curiosity informed by data.

However, the most significant innovation he observed was not a tool or platform but feedback loops of analytics. These were loops that made each project a learning organism.

The data that was generated when a project was completed was not lost in archives. It tested into its predictive models within the company which refined future estimates, resource-allocation algorithms, as well as improved risk simulations. Every project was smarter than the other with time. This perpetuated process of measurement, reflection, and improvement turned out to be the motor of organizational change.

John remembered that one of his teams applied this principle to reduce delivery times. The five years of project evidence that they examined included frequency of communication to budget variance and discovered that the more the analytics feedback loop was shorter, the higher the completion rate of project on time was 27 per cent. Based upon that understanding, they launched real-time reporting cycles and minimized delays within the portfolio.

What distinguishes between the digital project management and data-driven leadership, according to John, was continuous improvement via analytics feedback.

He made a sip of the coffee and smiled at the thought of his younger brother, who was once in fear that technology could take his place. It turned out he was wrong and the opposite was the truth. Analytics did not undermine the human position; it had made it higher. It relieved managers of the nightmare of exhausting reporting and speculation, leaving them to strategy, ingenuity and teamwork.

He envisaged the future as not being more technology but smarter integration. IoT sensors would increase real time visibility. AI would become prescriptive, as well as predictive, which would not only be forecasting but also making optimized decisions. Blockchain would also advance further to procurement to contract compliance and risk management. The analytics would be integrated with fintech to offer self-correcting budgets, and the ERP systems would develop into project-intelligence systems.

Nevertheless, the true change would be brought about by human adaptation, that is, organizations that would be humble enough to learn through information and brave enough to change due to it.

On this event, John had prepared a keynote at an international meeting on project-management. His subject was Future of Data Analytics in Project Leadership. When he concluded his notes he left one more fragment at the bottom of his outline, a message which he hoped he should close his speech with:

The future of project management is not about project management, but about intelligence management. Data does not only inform us about what we have been doing, it reflects on the kind of person we are becoming. Each impression is a reflection; each form a prototype. A future project manager is not a coordinator or a scheduler he is an interpreter of truth and a strategist of change and a keeper of progress.

On the following day, John was standing on the stage in front of project leaders all over the world and the burden of that truth was on him. A huge screen behind him visualized in real time large project analytics networks, millions of data points, which pulse with people, systems, and possibilities as they interconnect in real time.

He started his speech with no numbers but with thanks. He said he has made his career learning how to make the uncertainty personalized and structured. What I have learned though is that it is not about structure but about learning that the strength resides. In a world where analytics is able to know what we are about to do, the most important skill we can possess is the readiness to inquire, What can we learn out of this?

The spectators were bending down and not merely listening but believing. They too were not immune to this change- a generation of project managers who exchanged the frozen charts with smart systems and who came to understand that progress is not a goal but a feedback of understanding and doing.

By the applause John did not feel that they were applauding him, but that they were tuning in to a common time. The future had come and it was vibrant and adaptive, and very human.

He was silent in satisfaction when he walked out of the stage. The profession which started in the days of spreadsheets had reached the days of smart systems. But the central theme of his work had never shifted: to lead people to their clarity, purpose, and progress.

The sun went down again outside the conference hall and the skyline was painted in gold and amber. John paused, smiling softly. The power, he said to himself, has been obtained by data to see farther. But wisdom - wisdom is what to do with what we see.

And that being said, he had turned to look back at the future, where all projects, decisions, and lessons would start and finish with the same thing to say: insight is the new leadership.

FINAL THOUGHTS

As we conclude this journey through Data Meets Decisions, we return to the core belief that started it all: Insight is the new leadership.

The tools and technologies discussed in these pages—from Python and SQL to Power BI and AI—are powerful, but they are merely instruments. The true power lies in your ability to wield them with purpose. As a project manager, your role is shifting from simply tracking progress to predicting outcomes and shaping strategy.

We hope this book has not only provided you with technical knowledge but has also ignited a curiosity to explore further. The data landscape will continue to change, but the need for clear, data-informed decision-making will only grow.

Take these lessons, apply them to your projects, and lead with confidence. The future belongs to those who can translate data into decisions.

ABOUT THE AUTHOR'S

Shariful Haque is a PMP-certified Technology Leader, Data Analyst, and distinguished Researcher specializing in the intersection of business analytics and digital strategy. Currently a Doctorate of Business Administration candidate in Los Angeles, he combines executive experience with rigorous academic inquiry.

As the former Chief Operating Officer and Chief Data & AI Officer at Tech Wania, Shariful led cross-functional teams to drive enterprise-level digital transformation and launch innovative AI products. His strategic expertise bridges the gap between complex data engineering and high-level business management.

A significant contributor to the business research field, Shariful has published extensively on AI-driven IT strategy, non-profit management, and organizational agility. He holds multiple design patents integrating block chain technology with workflow systems and serves on the advisory boards of several international research organizations. He is a Senior Member of IEEE and a recipient of the Global Recognition Award for Transformative Data-Driven Leadership.

Kazi Sanwarul Azim is an experienced professional with a strong background in project management, business systems, and data analysis. Throughout his career, he has contributed to several major projects, supporting organizations in improving operations, streamlining processes, and making informed business decisions. His work includes coordinating cross-functional teams, managing product and supply-chain activities, analyzing performance data, and supporting technology-driven improvements across different business functions. Kazi is currently completing his Doctor of Business Administration at International American University in Los Angeles, where his research focuses on data management, digital transformation, and the role of analytics in modern organizations. He has published multiple research papers on topics such as artificial intelligence, FinTech, business intelligence, and data-driven performance improvement, receiving recognition for excellence in academic contribution. He brings a practical and research-based perspective to this book, aiming to help readers understand data management in a simple, useful, and real-world way.

Dhiraj Kumar is an accomplished data engineer and technology strategist with extensive experience across the healthcare, logistics, and insurance sectors. A trusted leader in designing scalable data ecosystems, he specializes in cloud architecture, machine learning pipelines, and large-scale ETL solutions. Dhiraj has architected robust platforms using medallion architecture and Unity Catalog governance, leading initiatives in FinOps cost optimization and secure data exchange. Known for his versatility in solution design and automation, he blends engineering excellence with business strategy, empowering organizations to solve complex problems and deliver reliable, enterprise-ready systems.

Khaled Al-Samad is a Doctoral Researcher at International American University (IAU), Los Angeles, CA, USA, pursuing a Doctor of Business Administration (DBA) with a concentration in Business Analytics.

He has over 18 years of multidisciplinary experience across shipbuilding, banking, beverage, garments, stock brokerage, sports shoe manufacturing, lubricant blending, energy and power, shipping, and textile industries. As a part-qualified public accountant under the Institute of Chartered Accountants of Bangladesh (ICAB), a learning partner of the Institute of Chartered Accountants in England and Wales (ICAEW), he brings deep expertise in accounting, auditing, financial reporting, and supply chain management. His doctoral research focuses on green shipping, maritime logistics, and data-driven decision-making, integrating AI and advanced analytics to improve corporate governance and sustainability outcomes.

MD Nadil Khan is a Senior Business System Analyst and a PhD candidate at the University of Cumberland, Department of Information Technology in Data Science.

He is known for significantly advancing healthcare through technology.

His work includes leading the successful implementation of an advanced Health Information System (HIS) and developing a proprietary telehealth platform, both of which have significantly enhanced healthcare accessibility and patient outcomes. Through his innovative use of data analytics and technology, Khan has driven advancements in personalized health solutions. His efforts in leveraging technology for healthcare improvements have not only improved operational efficiency but also set new standards for personalized care, making a significant impact on health and wellness accessibility.

MD Mohaiminul Hasan is a business technology professional and emerging AI researcher whose work focuses on data analytics, automation, and intelligent decision systems.

His award-winning publications explore Human–AI collaboration, digital marketing intelligence, and secure cloud solutions. With a strong background in business systems analysis and IT project management, he is committed to helping organizations use technology more efficiently and ethically.

Nur Mohammad is a distinguished Information Technology Expert and Senior Member of IEEE based in Los Angeles, California. Currently a Doctorate of Business Administration (DBA) candidate at Westcliff University, where he also earned his Master's in Information Technology, Nur combines academic rigor with extensive industry leadership. As the CEO of Scientific Editing & Publication Assistance and Tech Wania, he spearheads research initiatives in Artificial Intelligence (AI), IoT, and cybersecurity, contributing findings to leading journals including IEEE Access. His expertise spans digital transformation, software Quality Assurance (QA), and predictive modeling. Additionally, serving as a Private Research Consultant for Open Gen LLC, he guides organizations in leveraging AI for operational excellence. A dedicated educator and mentor, Nur has authored comprehensive courses on AI/ML and IT project management. He is an active member of the ACM and serves as the Secretary of Education for the Bangladeshi International Students Association of California (BISAC).

Roksana Akter is a dynamic business professional done an MBA and is pursuing a Master's degree specializing in Cyber Security at California State University, San Bernardino. With a strong foundation in accounting and financial management.

She holds a Bachelor of Business Administration and previously served as an Accountant at Al Amin Trading, where she managed complex financial reporting and forecasting. Currently based in Los Angeles, Roksana applies her leadership skills as an operations lead for the LA Community Space Food Bank, overseeing logistics and volunteer coordination. A recipient of the Dean's List and Best Teacher Award honors, she combines analytical precision with a committed approach to operational excellence and organizational growth.

Made in the USA
Monee, IL
04 November 2026

67386630R00134